SAGE was founded in 1965 by Sara Miller McCune to support the dissemination of usable knowledge by publishing innovative and high-quality research and teaching content. Today, we publish over 900 journals, including those of more than 400 learned societies, more than 800 new books per year, and a growing range of library products including archives, data, case studies, reports, and video. SAGE remains majority-owned by our founder, and after Sara's lifetime will become owned by a charitable trust that secures our continued independence.

Los Angeles | London | New Delhi | Singapore | Washington DC | Melbourne

IN THE SHADOW OF A SWORD

IN THE SHADOW OF A SWORD

THE MEMOIR OF A WOMAN LEADER IN THE LTTE

THAMIZHINI

TRANSLATED BY NEDRA RODRIGO

Los Angeles | London | New Delhi
Singapore | Washington DC | Melbourne

Copyright © Mahadevan Jayakumaran, 2021

Originally published in February 2016 in Tamil by Kalachuvadu Publications as *Oru kuurvaaLin Nizhalil*.

All rights reserved. No part of this book may be reproduced or utilized in any form or by any means, electronic or mechanical, including photocopying, recording, or by any information storage or retrieval system, without permission in writing from the publisher.

This translation published in 2021 by

SAGE Publications India Pvt Ltd
B1/I-1 Mohan Cooperative Industrial Area
Mathura Road, New Delhi 110 044, India
www.sagepub.in

YODA Press
79, Gulmohar Enclave
New Delhi 110049
www.yodapress.co.in

SAGE Publications Inc
2455 Teller Road
Thousand Oaks, California 91320, USA

SAGE Publications Ltd
1 Oliver's Yard, 55 City Road
London EC1Y 1SP, United Kingdom

SAGE Publications Asia-Pacific Pte Ltd
18 Cross Street #10-10/11/12
China Square Central
Singapore 048423

Published by Vivek Mehra for SAGE Publications India Pvt. Ltd. Typeset in 11/13 pt Adobe Caslon Pro by Fidus Design Pvt. Ltd, Chandigarh.

Library of Congress Control Number: 2020948205

ISBN: 978-93-5388-683-7 (PB)

SAGE YODA Team: Arpita Das, Ishita Gupta, Tanya Singh, Amrita Dutta and Neena Ganjoo

*For all those who lost their
lives in the war on the island
of Sri Lanka ...*

Thank you for choosing a SAGE product!
If you have any comment, observation or feedback,
I would like to personally hear from you.

Please write to me at **contactceo@sagepub.in**

Vivek Mehra, Managing Director and CEO, SAGE India.

Bulk Sales

SAGE India offers special discounts
for purchase of books in bulk.
We also make available special imprints
and excerpts from our books on demand.

For orders and enquiries, write to us at

Marketing Department
SAGE Publications India Pvt Ltd
B1/I-1, Mohan Cooperative Industrial Area
Mathura Road, Post Bag 7
New Delhi 110044, India

E-mail us at **marketing@sagepub.in**

Subscribe to our mailing list
Write to **marketing@sagepub.in**

This book is also available as an e-book.

CONTENTS

Foreword: Writing Life, Writing War by R. Cheran   ix
Translator's Preface: The Woman Who Refused to Die   xiii
Acknowledgements   xvii
Introduction   xviv

1. The Road Opened   1
2. I Was Born into War   29
3. The Political Cadre Undergoes Combat Training   43
4. The Tamil People and the Armed Conflict   61
5. The Female Fighter and an Unchanged Society   75
6. Memories of the Eastern Soil   85
7. A False Peace and Disrupted Civilian Life   101
8. We Lay Down Our Arms   123
9. Surrender and the Prison Cell   155
10. Rehabilitation   183

Glossary   195
About the Author   199
About the Translator   201

FOREWORD

Writing Life, Writing War

Let me begin with a personal note: I never had a chance of meeting her. However, some of my fellow editors of the weekly newspaper I edited during 1990–2001 were in touch with her off and on. In April or May 2015, I received a Facebook friend request from someone named Romila Jeyan. When I checked the profile and postings, I was not sure about the identity, ideological pinning and affiliation of the person. But I noticed a few poems. I ignored the request. A few days later I received a message from Romila Jeyan saying that she was Thamizhini and wanted me to read her poems as she was an 'avid' reader of my poetry. That's how our digital friendship began.

That was perhaps the period after her release, and she was fully engaged in writing. She and I became friends and several other Tamil writers, academics and artists became friends with her. I suggested to her that she should think about either writing about her life or to give a long interview about her experiences. It was way too early, she said. She preferred to write fiction and poetry. Some of the poems she shared with me were translated into English and appeared in the journal *City: The Journal of South Asian Literature* in 2017. In one of those communications she said she was planning to write her life story. There were no communications for a while. Then a note of apology arrived in my inbox saying she was sick and was out of communications. I received two more poems later, but she disappeared from digital communication. On 18 October 2015, I woke to the sad and shocking news that she had passed away. She had never told me that she was suffering from cancer.

I prefer to call this book Thamizhini's life writing, and not Thamizhini's memoir. Life writing is a designatory term and concept that initially emerged in feminist and postcolonial studies. As an inclusive term, I suggest life writing can include several modes of narratives. It challenges the usual generic boundaries between history, fiction, documentary, autobiography, oral testimony, diaries, letters, and digital writings. Life writing is also story-telling and poetry. It can both be personal and communal and is engaged with life's broad themes; while memoir is narrow, focused primarily on just one dimension of experience.

There are other remarkable works by Thamizhini. A short story collection, *mazhaikkaala iravu*, was published posthumously in 2017. She wrote several articles for the LTTE women's journal *suthanthira paravaikal* under her earlier name Chandrika. There are several poems yet to be collected and published. *In the Shadow of a Sword* is just one part of her creative oeuvre.

Unlike many other commercially published life writings and memoirs, this is not a 'Trauma to Triumph' narrative. It is partly a recollection of pain and tragedy, partly a project of redemption and partly an introspection of life as a militant feminist and an important leader of the Liberation Tigers of Tamil Eelam (LTTE), widely known as the Tamil Tigers. Sadly, Thamizhini did not live to see her memoirs and other literary works published in print. After the end of the war in May 2009, she was taken into custody by the Sri Lankan military, confined in 'rehabilitation' camps and released in 2013—a saga she vividly narrates in this chronological narrative. Except for a few factual errors, there are neither embellishments nor inventions in this story.

During the peace talks between the Government of Sri Lanka (GOSL) and the LTTE, facilitated by the Norwegian government between 2002 and 2005, a handful of the LTTE senior leaders became delegates to various conferences, talks, workshops and other exercises in the art of 'peace-making'. It was during this time that Thamizhini, as a leader of the women's wing of the LTTE, began meeting different groups of people. She was a well read, articulate, charismatic and powerful communicator. She interacted with Sri Lanka's Sinhala feminists', other activists and scholars at that time. Her impact on Sri Lanka's southern liberal polity was significant. She was the chief of the LTTE representatives in the Subcommittee on Gender Issues (SGI) set up by the

GOSL and the LTTE to address the issues and representation of women in the peace process. Dr Kumari Jayawardena, an eminent political scientist and doyen of Sri Lanka's women's movement, led the Sri Lankan government representatives. This was part of the reason why there was so much sympathy for Thamizhini and commemoration of her life after her untimely and tragic death by cancer in October 2015. The Sinhala translation of her book published in 2016 was a bestseller with at least three editions.

I still remember one of her long interviews that appeared in a Tamil weekly during the peace talks. She was asked to comment on the future of women's representation and issues of gender within the LTTE. Her response was striking: 'As long as Annai [Prabhakaran, the LTTE chief] is alive and leads, we will have no problem. He understands and supports our autonomy. But, I am afraid it will not be the case after him.'

These remarks clearly highlight the ideological and structural deficiency within the militant movement. They also portend the uneasy relationship between women's agency and empowerment in national liberation and nationalist struggles all over the world. As she further indicates in her writings, female militancy both unsettles and reinforces gendered binaries of nationalistic militarism. Empowerment for women in the context of militancy is a fragile and complex process, for which Thamizhini's life and writings are important testimonials.

In the Shadow of a Sword, in a sense, is also a critical look at the past, liberally splattered with bitterness, a fact that critics of her book in the Tamil context tend to emphasize. Some of her former militant colleagues, and critics, claim that Thamizhini failed specifically to 'own up' to her role in conscription during the last stages of the war and did not write about the sacrifice and valour of the LTTE. What her critics fail to understand is that ideological consistency may not be a virtue in the context of politico-military movements. History and political contexts do not follow our preferred or desired trajectories. It is rather unfortunate that Thamizhini did not have much time to reflect on all her experiences. She was terminally ill.

Life writing is a messy affair. There are moral and ethical dilemmas a writer must negotiate. Remembering all the details and contexts are not always possible for everyone. The latter parts of Thamizhini's book reflect an urgency to finish, a kind of race against time. We will never know how Thamizhini would have reacted to the shadows of sword in the hand of the Sri Lankan lion, guns and grenades of the soldiers and the near total militarization of Sri Lanka now.

Thamizhini's writing should also be viewed in the context of a burgeoning post-war corpus of Tamil auto-fiction, poetry, memoirs, novels, short stories and testimonies, including digital ones. This is a powerful literary movement, what I call 'Writing Genocide' as opposed to 'War Literature'. Although a significant amount of poetry and narratives are available in English, a large corpus of immensely sensitive and great work in Tamil is not to be found in English. Poet and translator, Nedra Rodrigo has been translating some of the key works of this genre. This book is one of her more important translations.

To know fully and record the past four decades of pain, horrors suffered and inflicted, resistance, disappointments, trauma and sacrifice is impossible. Thamizhini's *In the Shadow of a Sword* is a tree, albeit an important tree offering sustenance. We still need to see the forest.

R. Cheran
Toronto, May 2020

TRANSLATOR'S PREFACE

The Woman Who Refused to Die

'I'm telling you, she should have taken the cyanide and died.' An abrupt response from someone who had asked me what I was translating right now. I asked him if he had read her memoir. He said he hadn't; he knew what had probably happened and he didn't want to read about it. No woman should have allowed that to happen to her. She should have killed herself instead. I tried to explain to him that this unnameable thing was not mentioned in the memoir, but he had already changed the topic and had moved on. Eighteen years of a woman's life. Almost half her lifetime spent in a struggle, and someone who had almost no knowledge of her felt able to decide whether she ought to have lived or died. I had heard variations of this from others and could not help but feel overwhelmed with a familiar sickening dread. She had quoted almost the exact words in her book. The women combatants who survived the war were repeatedly told they should have died. They had no place in society, and their lives after the war had no value. Thamizhini was a woman with the temerity to choose to live.

Looking at her life in context, in the natural environment she observes with such care, in the loving family she abandons for the struggle and in the family she creates for herself, among her comrades, Thamizhini is not so easily dismissed. Behind the piercing gaze of her photos is a reflexive intellect that seems focused on something beyond the present. From the first words of her memoir[1] the reader is plunged into a narrative that is both observation and critical commentary, underpinned by a deep sense of accountability

---

[1] I acknowledge that in his introduction Prof. R. Cheran reads this narrative as life writing. I read it as memoir from the position that the genre can be deconstructed to allow for the inclusion of poetics and communal experience. These readings may exist beside each other to allow for a plurality of interpretation.

to the people, the land, and her fellow fighters, especially the women combatants.

In the Shadow of a Sword embeds us in the natural world, the terrain, of a Tamil homeland. What could be called a sense of environmental accountability arises from a tradition of interconnectedness between the Tamil language and the natural world dating from the Sangam period. In introducing the reader to the trees, birds and animals finding respite during ceasefire, Thamizhini reminds us of the impact of war on the natural world. When she writes of the combatants longing for their loved ones, referencing the *Tinai* (landscape) genre of *mullai* (forest), she creates a cultural space within the forest. Unlike the implicit understanding of reunification in the *mullai* genre, the hopes of the combatants to be reunited with their loved ones are futile, as they 'reach the end of their lives between the roots of the Vanni trees'. The landscape of Vanni is forest, but it can also turn into *paalai* (desert) during the summer droughts and requires native knowledge of the terrain for successful battle. In referencing *paalai*, the memoir foreshadows the loss and destruction that will occur in the battlefield of Vanni. This is made more poignant when Thamizhini recounts the use of drones to map this landscape. An instrument of war that spies on an unfamiliar terrain to conquer it, empties the terrain of its traditional, historical knowledge and its native inhabitants. In these passages she mourns her lost comrades, the destruction of nature, and the loss of heritage in profound and nuanced ways.

In the Shadow of a Sword is also an archive of the women who served in the LTTE, and here the duality of the word 'nizhal', which I have translated as shadow, but can also mean shade or shelter, is significant. In documenting the everyday lives of the rebels, and in speaking of the lives and motivations of women combatants, the memoir inserts these women into history. Though she came from a literate family that valued critical thought, Thamizhini gains a wider political education in the LTTE, which provides respite and nurturing (shelter) for her intellectual growth. As Thamizhini points out, it is through the Movement that many young women are afforded some respect and prestige. In her attention to the gendered violence normalized by war, she describes the entry of women combatants into the battlefield as a natural extension of their struggles against oppressive forces. Living with the threat of economic hardship, death, and sexual assault, turning to combat was a means of defence and resistance. It is also a means whereby they can be of service to their community. From her own experiences, in the opportunities the LTTE provides to serve the people, Thamizhini finds a vocation and a great sense of fulfilment.

The word 'nizhal' understood as shadow deserves the reader's attention as well. In her observations on blind adherence to a chain of command leading to disintegration of morale and a loss of integrity, Thamizhini critiques a nationalist movement that stunts its own growth in the service of an armed struggle. The intellectual and political underpinnings of the Tamil struggle wither under the monopoly of a single group, and under the conditions of a protracted, brutal war. But even as she holds herself and LTTE accountable for their decisions and actions, she also turns her gaze to the community she loves and feels abandoned by. She is critical of a society that was willing to accept women in the role of combatants but reverts to a chauvinist disposal of these same women when they survive the war. These critiques bring us to the questions of accountability and who this memoir was written for. Thamizhini maintains in her introduction that she writes this account for the people she dearly loved. As such, her willingness to turn the critique inward presents the reader with a model of accountability that is yet to be encountered in the narratives of the state after the war.

During her time in the rehabilitation camp, when Thamizhini hears some of the criticisms being levelled against her, she says: 'I learned to weigh people's intentions by seeing where the criticisms came from, and on what basis they criticized me.... I began to feel determined that just as the eagle renewed itself and arose to fly with new strength, I too would strengthen myself.' It is remarkable that after the experiences she had been through, in spite of the slander directed at her, even as she knew she was close to death, she chose to write her memoir in this form. It speaks to a renewal of a Tamil struggle through peaceful means, and a commitment to the survival and intellectual growth of the next generation.

Where Tamil experiences which contradict the narratives of the state are dismissed, with the taint of terrorism as an alibi, Thamizhini's memoir revives Tamil history, especially pertaining to women, and reinstates it into the body politic. Her words are a dirge that speaks meaning into the empty and silent spaces that remain after war.

Nedra Rodrigo
Toronto, 2020

ACKNOWLEDGEMENTS

I am immensely grateful to R. Cheran, K. Sundaram and the wonderful women at Yoda Press for trusting me with the translation of this valuable text. I also owe many thanks to poet Karunakaran, Paul (most supportive of partners), the York Centre for Asian Research for the support and space to ask difficult questions, Nimmi Gowrinathan for new critical spaces, the Tamil Symposium Collective, the Noolaham Foundation, my siblings and my wonderful global Tam Fam who keep me inspired and awake.

For the women who fly against the wind, may we remember your names.

INTRODUCTION

I have recorded here my memories of my journey through the fight, and the experiences it brought me. I cannot say that this is a complete history. It does not seem to be such a simple task to try and accurately record the incidents of a life that was thrust into war with the momentum of a forest flood that overflowed its banks from the moment I came into consciousness. All the same, I have poured out some of the fire that has burned in my heart as a barrier that cannot be wiped from the memory. That is all.

I have asked myself several times why I had to write this. Only one answer motivated me. I must tell the people I love as my life a few truths. The struggle that was conceived to redeem the political aspirations of a race, was built on thousands upon thousands of lives. Why did its course finally come to nothing? This is a question that has shaken the world.

I have been a member of the Liberation Tigers, who took control of the entire struggle. I have also lived as a witness to the latter 20 years of the struggle. We failed to protect our people. We lost our political ambitions while trying to protect our weapons. Today, our people's lives have been set back by two hundred years. They are regressing and shrinking into themselves as a people who trust nothing, fear everything, and are unable to succeed in the real world. Our generation still bears in their hearts the scars of a war that dragged on for 35 years.

All life-forms must struggle to survive. This is the law of nature. In the same way, our people must fight for their political rights. But I say from my soul that the next generation should not have to go down the road of an armed struggle. There should not be another river of blood in this country. No mother should weep while beating the belly that bore her child, or the coffin that carries her child. Our future generations must win over the world through their intellectual work. They must know for themselves the visions of a modern world of united minds. Every hero who gave their lives on the battlefield thought to themselves, let this war end with us; none of them hoped to see it continue to the next generation.

The lessons of the past must guide our generation to a strong and victorious path. I do not know if I have effectively passed on the message that I hope to share with the people of this country, and future generations. But I have tried hard to do so. I became a fighter because of a strong desire from my student days to do some good for the society to which I belonged. My life will be that of a fighter to the end. My experiences have taught me that I cannot do any good for my community, my country, or the world by taking up weapons, or by seeking revenge. Only patience and peace can create favourable conditions for the growth of any society. Thereby, my battle will continue for peace and tranquility for my community, my country and for the world, until my final days.

I am aware that the path to true peace is harder than the road to war. This book emphasizes the need for initiatives to overcome the many obstacles to that progress. I raise my hands in the confidence that thousands of fighters for peace, who have true love for humanity and true community feeling, will link their hands in mine, and stand with me.

—Thamizhini

1

The Road Opened

It was February, in the year 2002. The rainy season had ended, the drizzle had eased off and the spring season had begun. The spreading forests of Vanni began to bud again in their abundance. The fragrance of blossoming flowers trembling on creepers that stretched out and wove through the great trees filled the air. Monkeys swung fearlessly off the uluvintham tree branches. Small iguanas left their burrows to roam about; wild hares quenched their thirst on dewdrops off patches of grass; wild peacocks spread out their tails gently shaking them to dry in the early morning sun, and jungle fowl and babblers set out in search of food; the constant loud tremors of exploding bombs, flames, and the smell of sulphur having ceased now, the forest of Vanni seemed to relax and bask in the serenity granted by the cessation of war.

When the Sri Lankan government and the Liberation Tigers came to a ceasefire in 2002, the first step was an agreement to reopen the A9 highway for public use. This road, which linked Kandy, in the central hill country, and the northern point of Jaffna town, was 325 kilometers long. It is considered one of the primary roads in Asia, and travels through many cities in Sri Lanka. From the time the Tamil Liberation groups took up arms against the Sri Lankan government troops, between 1984 and 2006, the road was closed to public traffic many times.

The road was to be reopened on 15 February 2002. Since about 20 per cent of the road was under the control of the Liberation

Tigers of Tamil Eelam, the occasion became a matter of international interest as well. Some of the other female cadres and I went to the town of Omanthai to participate in the event, on behalf of the Women's Political Wing of the Tigers. The Deputy Head of the Political Wing, Sutha (Thangan), Head of the LTTE Peace Secretariat, Pulithevan, as well as other fighters participated in the event. The Sri Lankan army defence troops and the Tigers' defence troops stood face to face. Between them the A9 was closed with sandbags and barricades. The road was opened for public use in the presence of some higher-ups from the International Ceasefire Monitors and the International Red Cross.

Across the road soaked in the blood of thousands, the army personnel stood crowded together, just like us. Though we all shook hands with them and smiled, our other hands still held on tightly to our weapons. At the time, all of us, including the Leader of the Movement, Prabhakaran, felt flushed with victory in the knowledge that the Sri Lankan government had agreed to discussions because of the LTTE's continued victories, and in the belief that we had finally gained international recognition.

The press was spread out and crowding into A9 road. Throughout the period of fighting, the press was completely denied permission to enter the Vanni battlefield by the Tigers and the army. When I saw the local and international press who had come there, I felt that the eyes of the world had turned towards us. We the Tigers, in our striped camouflage, bearing arms, were besieged by the 'click click' of flashing cameras, the video equipment, extended microphones and recording equipment.

The media began barraging us with questions. But all the questions seemed to have the same basic purpose. It seemed that they were attempting to get their own predetermined answers out of the fighters' mouths.

'You were militants, why have you come to a peace process? Have you given up on Tamil Eelam? After thousands of your fighters have died for the cause, will you accept it if your leader abandons Tamil Eelam? Will there be more fighting? Do you have faith in this peace process? Will you go to war again? Don't you want to go back home? Will you fall in love? Will you get married? Will the Movement give you permission for this? Why do you twist your braids like this? Why are you wearing a holster? What's the difference between you and the women in the community? Do you think your society will accept you again?' A hundred questions were hurled at the fighters.

The media strategy seemed to go beyond the official news and the announcements made by the Movement's Head Secretariat, to pry into the everyday mind-frame of ordinary fighters and the middle-tier leadership. Only a select few from the Movement were given permission to answer the media's queries. So, when they found themselves in these situations, many fighters would smile and try to slip away. At the ceremonial reopening of the A9, Thangan, Pulithevan and I had been permitted to give answers to the participating media. Peace having returned to them after a long time, the opening of the road, and the lifting of the embargo seemed to bring a new light to people's faces. Yet, in what was generally spoken, I couldn't hear any faith in the Tigers' ability to move forward to maintain the peace and come to a permanent settlement. On the contrary, the people seemed anxious that the peace could end at any time and persisted with the intention of improving their lives by whatever means they could in the time they had. Both the Sri Lankan government and the Tigers had always acted with an understanding of the strategic military and political benefits of holding the A9, which ran through many Tamil areas, under their own control. As a result, the lives lost in the terrible battles that took place near that road numbered in the thousands. I think it's important to expand on this time by returning to events I directly participated in between 1995 to 2002.

After the Sri Lankan military had completely seized Jaffna district in December of 1995, the Liberation Tigers Movement had made the mainland of Vanni their primary base of operations. During that time, the Tigers could not reconcile themselves to the loss of Jaffna. Jaffna had not only been the base for recruitment and the growth of the Movement, but also the stronghold of trade. From 1990, it had been the official headquarters for the Tigers. Both the political leader Thamilselvan and Head of the finance division Thamizhenthi often spoke passionately to the fighters on the impact of the loss of Jaffna. The Tigers began to act with a firm resolve to seize back Jaffna very soon.

Both male and female cadres who knew the areas of Jaffna district well were selected for a brigade that was created to go to Jaffna. Lt. Col. Mahenthi and Lt. Col. Thanikaichelvi were both appointed to lead those troops. The Tigers began operations for disruptive attacks on the military stationed in Jaffna holding Poonakari as its rear base. The political leader Thamilselvan also headed these attacks. He had gained the admiration of the Leader by distinguishing himself in a successful attack on the Indian Army in Thenmaradchi, with a very small troop. After that, until he was appointed political leader in 1993, he held the position of military captain of Jaffna district under the name of Dinesh.

The Head of the Movement's finance division, Thamizhenthi, had been emotionally affected a great deal by the loss of Jaffna. When he spoke at a gathering of leaders and cadres, he explained the financial crisis facing the Movement. He said that the everyday rations, clothing, equipment and medical expenses needed for the fighters required a monthly expenditure of millions of rupees. 'The Movement can't afford to properly feed the fighters who give their lives to battle every day,' he said through his tears. His words deeply moved those present. In the following period he established the foundations for the great agricultural projects in the Vanni areas, but he also began the taxation system that became the cause of great resentment among the civilians towards the Tigers' organization.

At that time, I was operating as the head of the women's political education division. I was put in charge of 20 female cadres who had received training in the 33rd troop at the women's training base established in Polikandy. Our base, which had been in the Kanakampuliyadi Junction in Thenmaradchi, was now changed to the Vaddakachchi agricultural farming complex. The political training school was also run out of that same complex. The education division gave lessons to the fighters, and to the injured who had been assigned to political duties. The meetings of the political cadres would also usually take place there. Political strategist Anton Balasingham, and Balakumaran, an important figure in the

Movement, ran political classes there. I too had taken a class titled 'Women and Society' there.

Our education division's task was to go to the frontlines and to the training bases to meet fighters and to educate them in politics, general knowledge, and the history of the Movement. Before 1995, the female brigade had functioned as a single administrative unit. The special captain held sole and complete authority over all the women in the female brigade. In the period following, the female brigade became the Malathi brigade, and was divided into various political, economic, intelligence and Sea Tiger units. Since I was able to travel to the frontlines where female brigades were posted, I came to understand many of the problems they faced. I also gave lessons in politics to the female Sea Tigers positioned on the beaches near the Vadamaradchi cove's training base.

On the 17th of July 1996, the Tigers gathered all their forces and launched a massive attack on the military base in Mullaitivu. The education division cadres and I were stationed in the medical base in the area beside the Mullaitivu colony. We had undertaken the task of stanching the bleeding for injured fighters and rushing them to the surgical units serving in the rearguard. Through this operation, called 'Unceasing Waves – 1', the entire base was captured by the Tigers. In the process, more than a thousand lost their lives, between the Tigers and the army. In the battlefield of Vanni, the first great battle victory was won by the Tigers on the shores of Nanthikadal in 1996. I went along with other cadres to the captured base. The great wide waves of the Bengal Sea pounded upon the shores of Mullaitivu, like parai drums testifying to the sacrifice of our fighters.

The Tigers, who had lost the deep ocean area of Vadamaradchi, took Mullaitivu as their primary naval base, and began a rigorous training of the Sea Tigers, under the premise that 'He who rules the sea, rules the land'. The Movement was adamant that the greater part of naval dominance around the island of Sri Lanka remain in their hands. Having gained the advantage of international sea routes in the Bengal Sea, they had the opportunity to purchase weaponry, mines and ammunition using their own ships. This advantage gave the Tigers' Movement a further edge in the continuing battle in Vanni. In the Sea Tiger brigades, female cadres ran their operations equally on the frontlines with their male counterparts.

Within a few days of the Tigers capturing Mullaitivu base, the Sri Lankan armed forces began 'Sath Jaya 1,2,3', the successive attempts to capture Kilinochchi town. We immediately had to move our education division, which was based in Vaddakachchi, to a more secure location. There was a training base for new fighters in that same complex. When their leader first came to my area there had been a hundred new recruits with him. He was agitated because he hadn't yet received any instructions on transporting the recruits and didn't know what to do. The Paranthan area was quaking under the heavy shelling. I didn't think it was right to leave the new recruits there, when they barely knew how to take measures to defend themselves. At that time, it was necessary for me to make that decision without approval from higher command. Though I knew I would have to face disciplinary action from the leadership if those new recruits' lives were endangered because of my choices, I made an executive decision with the intention of saving their lives.

Since the basic training camp administration hadn't taken office yet, the fighters had not yet received their training uniforms. They were in the same state as when they'd left home. It was evening then, and I thought it wouldn't be too hard to take them in those clothes on the road. I mixed in the 20 fighters who were with me among them and split them into small teams. We couldn't wait around for vehicles at this point of crisis. So, having decided to take them walking along the road, I broke them up into smaller groups and sent them off in the front street of the Vaddakachchi Maha Vidyalayam. In this way we passed the road beneath the Iranamadu tank area and reached the Iranamadu junction. We took the A9 main road and resumed our journey on foot towards Murikandy. We walked, with the intention that once we reached Murikandy, we could leave the A9 and take a forest path to reach the Akkarayan section of the forest beyond the range of the shelling. The new fighters had come running and walking and were soaked in sweat. Some of them were terrified because the shelling was so close. As we were walking from Murikandy Junction toward the road to Akkarayan, in the area just beside Union pond, we were pleased to see female fighters from the Political Wing who had set up a tent there. Vino, a female fighter I knew very well, was left in charge of the station. With her assistance we had the new fighters stay the night in a relatively safe section of the forest. Vino cooked some dinner for us with the help of some of the neighbouring residents.

The next morning, the head of our Women's Political Wing, Lt. Col. Tharani arrived there. She made the arrangements for the recruits to be sent to a training base and gave instructions for our education division to be assigned a safe base. She also told us that the army had captured some significant posts in the Paranthan area in the previous night's battle. We could not return to the Vaddakkachchi complex again; it had become a danger zone. If you wanted to choose an appropriate place to set up a base in Vanni, you would have to know the geography and layout of the area very well. Because some places may have water sources, and others might not. No matter how deep you dug a well, you might not find water. Not only that, while it could be parched and dried up in the summer months, in the cold months it could look like a pond with all the flooding. The head of the men's education division and I decided on a spot in a rural area called Kollar, Puliyankulam. Though it was partly in the forest, the forest here was not as dense. On the contrary, it had some great trees and some areas of shrubbery here and there. There were small wells in between. We set up our bases near those existing wells. There were no dwellings around us. Only the family of the priest who performed pooja in the small temple nearby, lived there. He had a large vegetable garden and a herd of cattle. He knew many things about the layout of the area, and he also maintained the small temple. Even people from distant areas would visit him on and off for 'magic paint' and protective amulets. He said that in earlier times, many people from outside areas would come there and engage in different forms of cultivation.

One day, as we were exercising at dawn in a small clearing near our base, about 10 to 15 deer came roaming leisurely around us.

We were all captivated by the deer, which seemed so regal and beautiful with their many-branched antlers. The fighters stopped their exercise so as not to disturb them and stood around admiring the deer. At that time, we were lost in a joy that made us forget the world. When we told the male cadres about this happening, they said: 'What an opportunity; if you had shot at least one deer we could have got some good meat.' 'You're always thinking about food,' said our female fighters and got into an argument with them.

Throughout 1997, operation 'Sath Jaya' continued in the Kilinochchi area. The Women's Political Wing also prepared themselves for attack. Our education division had been joined with the attack division. I was given charge of a team of 30 fighters. Our team was assigned attack exercises in the area beside Uruthirapuram Hindu College. The environment of that school stirred strong memories of my early school days. I had represented my school in several competitions at Hindu College. I had played in many volleyball tournaments in that playground. I had participated in many debates, speech contests, and theatrical productions on the stage in the great hall and won prizes.

It must have been in 1990 or 1991. An A-level student was killed when he was caught in an aerial bombing carried out on the playing field behind the school. That student, Sathyaseelan, had been in my afternoon class. His death had triggered an outpouring of emotion among us students.

By 1997, my birthplace of Paranthan had become a terrifying war zone. I couldn't even find out where my family was. I thought they might have gone to Skandapuram or Tharmapuram. It was painful to think that my family, who had been so dependent on farming for their livelihood, might be displaced and unable to even feed themselves. The schools empty without students, the desolate streets, and the paddy fields overgrown with patches of grass made me despair. I firmly believed that if the people were to return to these places, and live peacefully here, we had to fight a war. At the time, I felt that if it came to it, I would be honoured to fight in battle and die in my own hometown.

Our troop was stationed in what was called the second block in the Paranthan Mullaitivu road. It was an exposed field with little cover, and the slightest movement could give us away to the army. Our fighters suffered injuries and casualties almost daily as a result of the short-range mortar shells we were bombarded with. So, we were entrusted with digging long trenches. We plugged away at the difficult work of guard duty at nighttime, and combat training and digging long defence trenches in the fields during the day. The army kept us under threat with the thundering of their moving battle tanks. During operation 'Sath Jaya', the army used the attack strategy of sending out their battle tanks ahead through the fields and dirt roads, followed by their troops. The female fighters of the rocket propelled grenade (RPG) heavy weapon division were stationed in our section to launch attacks on the battle tanks and halt their progress.

At night, we also needed to send out small teams beyond our vanguard defence to position themselves beside the army defence and spy on the army's nocturnal movements. If we saw the army edging forward at night, we needed to launch a counter strike immediately. Our vanguard defence had to be ready in an instant to attack and quash their progress. During this time, the surveillance teams had to run back quickly and join up with our station. If there was any hesitation at this stage, they would be caught in the crossfire and lose their lives.

My troop was also often sent out on these reconnaissance missions. One day, my team took cover in the shelter of some portia trees beside the YMCA building on Murasumoddai Street. The army searchlights were as bright as midday. We lay low on the ground, unable to so much as raise our heads. Around us, the bushes, shrubs and vines were parched by the dry season. The army was hurling grenades, and suddenly the shrubs caught fire, combusting 'sada sada' around us. Not knowing what else to do at the time, we huddled around a portia tree and broke off its tender branches. We crept through an area where there were fewer flames, escaped that firetrap and scampered. The army must have heard some unusual sound. For a while, in addition to a heavy weapon assault, they also fired two or three mortar shells at us. One of the fighters who went with me returned with a burn on her arm, that was it. The fighters on our defence fortification later told us that when they had seen that fire blazing, they figured there was no chance we'd return alive.

Another time, after we were engulfed in pitch darkness, we were suddenly informed that we had to move and station our troops slightly further ahead. We were put on full alert in anticipation that the army could start advancing early the next morning. The distance between our troop and the army was extremely short. In conditions where the light of a firefly could provoke a volley of fire, closed in by the dark, so close we were brushing against each other as we moved, we managed to reach the identified location and stationed our troop there. I was set up near a small ditch. After organizing the defence posts, I spread out a sleeping bag to try and get some rest. As soon as I lay down, I felt something slip and slither near my shoulders. So as not to spread any panic, I gently nudged Arachelvi, a fighter who was lying down next to me. 'I'll get up slowly. Use your flashlight, covering it as much as possible with a cloth, and look around the ground near my shoulders to see what's there,' I said as I rose up. There, glistening and gleaming silver, was a large snake, slithering into its coils. They say: 'a battalion trembles on seeing a snake', what of me alone? The hairs rose on my flesh, and I felt dizzy. We huddled together immediately to figure out what to do. We couldn't kill the snake now without endangering everyone. So, we shoved it into a bunker, sealed the opening so it could not escape and freed it the next day.

As I was engaged on the frontline, I received word that I was to go to the rearguard. Lt. Col. Thanikaichelvi told me that we must do the work that the Movement requires from us when it is asked and sent me on to the rearguard. The head of the Political Wing, Thamilselvan said that we needed to take the future needs of the Movement into consideration and appoint female combatants to the Political Wing; he wanted me to take on the responsibility of guiding that project. In keeping with that, some girls with some basic knowledge of English were selected to be educated further in English, as well as to receive some training in politics and computer science. In addition to the work with the education division, I was given the responsibility of taking care of the administrative work as well.

During 1997–98, many public organizations were created by the heads of the political departments in each district, to work among the civilians. Many of the Movement's tasks were carried out with great enthusiasm and cooperation by civilians, through the organization known as the Revolutionary Committee. Step by step, the people's organizations began to be linked to activities close to the war effort, by making announcements about the Movement's meetings and recruiting people and organizing the events commemorating the Heroes' deaths. At the same time, the campaigning segment of the Political Wing also began furiously recruiting people for the Movement. Conferences on contemporary politics were continuously held at municipal and district levels. The idea of everyone participating in the war effort was wholeheartedly taken up and developed in street theatre and music events. The propaganda was heightened in places where young men and women gathered. Since my name was included in the list of speakers of the Political Wing, I was often called upon to speak at many gatherings. At the same time, I had to go around to a number of places setting up classes for the fighters on the frontlines, as well as for the fighters in the basic training camps. I was given an MD90 motorcycle that could run on kerosene, for my own use. A large part of my life as a fighter was spent on the road first in Jaffna district, and later in the Vanni plains.

On the 13th of May 1997, the Sri Lankan army began operation 'Jayasikuru', with the intention of completely capturing the Vanni area. This operation was undertaken on two fronts: one in the Manal Aru district through Nedunkeni, and the other in Vavuniya near the A9, through Omanthai. The Liberation Tigers rustled up their entire fighting strength and confronted it with a roar of 'do or die'. In this period of two and a half years, the female brigades also played a significant role. 'Malathi Brigade', which held the fighters with the most combat experience, performed with unparalleled valour during the time of 'Jayasikuru'.

The Leader created a new female brigade in the name of Major Sothiya with fighters who had received their basic training in the Ambakamam forest area of Vanni. Sothiya was born in Jaffna's Karaveddy district. She had received her training in Tamil Nadu and had grown as a fighter skilled in battle operations and efficient in her administrative work as well. She had begun as a medical officer and was later appointed first special commander of the women's brigade by the Leader. She died of an illness on the 11 January 1990 in the Manal Aru forest area. Her body was interned at the Kilali women's training base and the base was named 'Major Sothiya Training Base'. I had received weapons training in this camp in 1992 in the 21st battalion of the women's brigade. This was the first weapons training base established in the North by the Liberation Tigers for the training of women.

Thurka was appointed the special brigadier of the Sothiya brigade. Basically, she too had begun as a medical officer, and was raised to the rank of attack brigadier. Major Sothiya's brigade was created as a special 'jungle command' unit and given specific jungle training. They were also given some priority in the Leader's circle of external guard.

At the time of quashing 'Jayasikuru', the role of the eastern province fighters was immeasurable. The Jayanthan and Anbarasi brigades travelled several hundred miles on foot through the jungles to take part in the battle. I had been to the Anbarasi brigade camp, which was stationed in Mulliyavalai's Puthanvalai district, several times to hold classes in politics. Many arts events and musical performances were held in the Mulliyavalai Rangan base. These eastern province fighters, heirs to the land of singing fish and honey, were incredibly talented. The Tamil they spoke, in their own unique style, full of lighthearted humour, was just beautiful. Many women in that camp became dear friends of mine. I can firmly say that without the hard work and sacrifice of the eastern province fighters, the Liberation Tigers would not have won as many battles as they did in the Vanni battlefield.

Many fighters called the time of 'Jayasikuru' 'porridge time'. A thin porridge made of a little rice and a lot of salted water was brought to the battlefront in plastic bags every day for the morning meal. A watery curry of beef or brinjals with rice in the afternoons, and at night some puttu and a watery tomato curry, filled the stomachs of the fighters engaged in the rigorous work of battle, but gave them little nourishment. So, on the frontlines, where the ground shook from time to time, the fighters were injured or killed in large numbers. At the same time, injured fighters were sent back to the frontlines even before their injuries were healed. There were times when a fighter who was injured 10 times was sent back into battle for the eleventh time. The medics were also worried that those who were suffering from massive blood loss were taking longer to heal because of malnourishment. As far as I knew, at least two fighters died of anemia.

The female fighters stood and fought in battle in tattered and faded clothes. A fighter named Aanthira, a friend of mine from the training base, showed me the state of her clothes when I had gone up to the frontline once. Her jeans were worn and tattered at the back. 'Hey, next time you come, somehow bring me a couple of things to wear,' she rightfully demanded of me. It was the same situation for the ones doing political work too. I have spoken on stage impeccably dressed in clothes that had faded at the back, which I had unpicked and re-sewn inside out and ironed. I prepared an outfit for Aanthira. Before I could take it to her, I heard the news of her Hero's death on the Tiger's Voice radio.

In the midst of all these hardships, the battle to defeat 'Jayasikuru' had become emotionally charged for the fighters. Some of the fighters who had worked with me in the education division were also involved in this battle. Of them, a fighter called Nithya had written in her last letter to me, 'This is not Puliyankulam, but the Lake of Uprising (Puratchi Kulam).' I would often travel to the 'Jayasikuru' frontlines and stay with the female cadres. The fighters who had set up camp in the dense jungle, and been fighting for years, were eager to hear news of the outside. Many of the fighters were in a state of limbo, not knowing where and how their family members were. 'We see nothing but these jungle trees. Tell us about the folks out there. If we die fighting in the jungle, who knows if our bodies would be returned to our mothers and fathers. Rain, mist, heat, all the seasons pass by us in this jungle.' There were many thousand stories like this, many deep sighs. Their stories and dreams are buried deep in the layers of my memory: all those who lived entirely in the jungle during the war, carved the names of their beloveds on its tree trunks, kept their tender loves behind their own eyes, buried their silent loves in their own hearts and reached the end of their lives between the roots of Vanni trees.

At this juncture, the Tamil civilians' condition was even worse than ours. They were tormented by being unable to get ordinary medicines, fuel and daily necessities because of the economic embargo imposed by the government, the constant displacement because of the war, and living in fear for their lives. Unable to take up any work, including farming, they clung to the meagre goods they were able to get with their ration cards, and the items they received from one or two NGOs as tokens of life, even as their lives were in limbo. The burden of everyday life battles of mother-child malnutrition, students abandoning their studies, the lack of regular medical facilities, all ground them down. As the world headed towards the peak of modernity in the 20th century, people in the Tiger-held areas reverted to the days of the bullock cart. However, we clung to the ingrained dream that if we somehow liberated our motherland, then we could reverse the brain drain, and raise our nation to the level of a nation like Singapore. That dream sustained us in the face of our people's suffering.

The Political Wing carried out a lot of work among the people. One segment of the Political Wing took on the title of 'Tamil People's Rehabilitation Division', and established a pediatric nutrition centre, student centres, pre-schools and centres to distribute food for children in the afternoon. On top of this, they also established accommodations for the displaced. The Political Wing stood firm that the Tamil People's Rehabilitation Division would serve as a guiding example to the NGOs in the Vanni area. Further than this, even though we set up a women's organization, student organization, and an economic development centre to undertake projects among the people, the lack of resources made it impossible to complete them. As a result, the Political Wing was reduced to the task of recruiting people for the Movement.

The 'war uprising team' was set up to begin giving the people training in self-defence. The plan was established to train everyone, whether villagers, businesspeople, women or students. At the same time, a civilian border patrol troop was created. Lt. Col. Anbu established an auxiliary team as reinforcements in Vanni, for the very first time. She had functioned as special commander of the troops stationed in the Manal Aru forest area during 1990–93. She was held in very high esteem and was greatly beloved among the fighters, as well as the people in Mulliyavalai, Kumulumunai, Alampil, Kokkilai, Kokkuthoduvai and Naayaaru areas. Anbu, who had the knowledge of the inner paths of the Manal Aru jungles at her fingertips, gave a select few civilians combat training, and engaged them as reinforcements and guides for the troops engaged in attack manoeuvres in the Manal Aru jungle, even stationing some of them in defence positions. Many of the civilians who took part in these attacks lost their lives. She demanded that the leadership give them the same honours as the Heroes who died in the battlefield and provide their families with some small financial help. This brave leader, Lt. Col. Anbu, who, for the first time in the history of the Movement, was able to recruit auxiliary reinforcements without any force but with wholehearted participation, died in the Poonakari battle in 1993. Her role in protecting a large section of the Tamil population in the Tamil-Sinhala border villages and preventing the military-assisted Sinhala colonization will be firmly planted in the history of the Tamil people.

During the 'Jayasikuru' clash, there was an attempt to reinstate a similar civilian-military organization in the Vanni battleground. This functioned as a border-patrol unit, organizationally separate under the Political Wing. A separate training camp was set up for the border patrol unit as well. The commencement event for this camp was held as a special ceremony at the Malathi Stadium in Puthukkudiyiruppu and began with the raising of the Tiger flag. I too participated in the event. I could hardly believe my eyes at the flood of thousands of people standing at attention. Karuna Amman, who led the vanguard brigade at the 'Jayasikuru' battle frontlines launched the ceremony. It was the aim of the Political Wing to inspire civilians to form a people's auxiliary army, like revolutionary Mao's Red Army, and lend their strength to leader Prabhakaran's military attacks.

With all avenues to a normal life shut off to them in the state of war, whether they liked it or not, the people had no choice but to go along with the words of the Tigers. During that period, I too worked vehemently in these undertakings as a propaganda officer. Only a small portion of the population participated wholeheartedly in the training and was prepared to go to the frontlines as part of the border patrol. A vast number of civilians, for lack of any other option, gave the appearance of participating willingly. Some refused right away and roundly condemned us. However, as more increasingly severe measures were put into practice, the circumstances arose where training became unavoidable. The leadership hoped that, though there was a shortage in numbers in the Movement at the time, stationing the civilian border patrol in the areas the Tigers had captured would prevent those areas from being lost, and put some psychological pressure on the Sri Lankan government and military. More than this, there was the intent in this effort, to show the world that the Liberation Tigers' battle was the people's battle.

All the civilians had to come to the training stadium. Only the elderly, those with heart diseases, the handicapped, pregnant women, breastfeeding women, and those with serious illnesses were exempt. Everyone else had to be trained and receive identification cards confirming that training. People without those identification cards were prevented from receiving any kind of help, even from the village officers. With no recourse, everyone began to participate in the training. Even my mother would pick up a spade handle and come to the nearby stadium for training. She told me that the instructor had asked her to walk around the stadium instead, because she had swelling and pain in both her knee joints.

Under those conditions, the battle in Vanni raged on multiple fronts. The great stretch of Vanni had been shrunken by war. The people were trapped in the horrors of war and they suffered. To the west of the A9, taking Mallavi as a centre, in the areas of Thunukkai, Yogapuram, Kalvilaan, Theraankandal, Jayapuram, Vellankulam, Mulankavil, Kiranchi, Akkarayankulam, Vannerikulam, and to the east of the A9, taking Puthukkudiyiruppu as a center, in the areas of Vaddakkachchi, Visuvamadu, Puliyampokkanai, Piramanthanaaru, Udayarkattu, Theraavil, Peraaru, Katsilaimadu, Keppapilavu, Kumulamunai and Alampll, they made their homes in small huts crowded together, and under spread out tarpaulin. Apart from the one or two broadcast stations set up by the LTTE's Intelligence Division, they had no other means of contact with the outside world.

The youth were absolutely forbidden from leaving Vanni. Only those who had received entry into universities to further their studies, and engaged women who were leaving for their weddings, as well as those with business or health emergencies, were allowed to leave, after showing sufficient documentation, and receiving permission from the Tigers' intelligence officers. Even so, some of the wealthy gave over their houses and properties to the Movement and left with their families. The procedures followed in the places where the Tigers dealt out permission for travel came under all kinds of criticism from the people. The cadres like us, who worked among the people, were forced to hang our heads unable to answer their angry questions. Though we were members of the Movement, we did not know the shortcomings of the organizational practices of the Movement as they did.

When we informed the officials of the people's questions and suspicions, and asked them for an explanation, we were told that the intelligence unit was sending a select few on secret missions to Colombo. There was some truth in that. However, many wealthy folks took advantage of those preparations to leave as well.

The people were more aware of these kinds of official malpractices than we were. As a result, they developed some bitterness and anger toward some of the Movement's institutions. We applied a temporary balm to the people's distress: 'Put up with these difficulties just a little longer, for the sake of national liberation; we'll soon win our homeland. Our leader will soon bring about an end to our problems.' Yet some of the actions and decisions of the Movement caused unease and seemed an unsolvable riddle to us fighters. It was the poor people, who had faced so many displacements, and suffered so many losses, who were now losing their lives as border patrollers and fighters on the battlefields. We, the fighters, still did not budge even a little from our belief that our leader Prabhakaran, who loved the people so much, would create a great future for them.

I experienced something unforgettable in the Mallavi area. An A-level student, who had been deeply stirred by the recruiting cadres and joined up, had been sent for training. One day, her father came to our camp. Unlike other parents, he did not scold us, or beg us to give him back his daughter. He came in a wheelchair, because his legs were paralysed. It was my task to face him, on behalf of the Movement. That father said to me: 'Sister, I am a beggar. I do some menial work and saved the money I got as charity to put my daughter through school; I'm not complaining that my daughter went to fight. Let her go; what goes for the town, goes for me. But, tomorrow, when all these doctors and engineers who have studied so well come back from overseas, my daughter and my family, who fought for the nation, will stand before them like uneducated beggars. That's what bothers me when I think about it.' Though I spoke all kinds of comforting words to that father, his complaint was planted as an unanswerable question in my heart. I never saw that father or daughter again, but my heart was tormented by the truths in his tearful words.

Our camp, which had been stationed in Kollar Puliyankulam, was moved to Puthukkudiyiruppu. All the organizations of the Movement took Puthukkudiyiruppu as their nucleus. All the fighters, including leader Prabhakaran, held on to the baseless belief that the Sri Lankan army would never take Puthukkudiyiruppu. Puthukkudiyiruppu was a high-level security enclosure, built with the most extreme security measures.

In 1998, the Leader entrusted the task of releasing the 'Freedom Birds' newspaper to me. Though I had had the opportunity to meet with him many times before, it was when we met over my responsibilities for 'Freedom Birds' that I had the opportunity to speak to him directly. He expected that I should make many changes in the newspaper. 'Women's problems should be brought forward by women. Men can talk about women's freedom better than women; even I could probably speak about feminism better than you could. But I am not able to fully understand your problems. No man can fully appreciate all the difficulties women undergo. Women must speak and write about women's issues. It will only be accurate then. It should be mostly women writing in "Freedom

Birds". The female cadres who have some writing skills should be found, and they should be given writing exercises, and have group discussions,' he noted.

There was a press called Malathi Publications in the care of the Political Wing. It was there that the 'Liberation Tigers' newspaper was also printed. When we didn't have a computer or offset printing resources in Vanni, each letter had to be arranged by hand, each image needed a block, which was an exhausting task in a time of shortages. Because newsprint paper had been banned, we had to get the necessary paper from the Political Wing. I was furiously involved in my administrative work for three of the Women's Fronts: the education team, 'Freedom Birds' and the Political Science division, while also carrying out my propaganda duties in different areas.

The eastern province cadres had been through many obstacles, clashed with the army in the dense jungle, walked long distances for many months and were arriving in Vanni to the 'Jayasikuru' frontline. At the same time, some troops were heading east from Vanni for some tasks. Under the leadership of the young commander Keeran, some women from the Political Wing, a few medical officers and others formed a unit to head towards Batticaloa.

It was at the end of 1998, or early in 1999. A month after this team had left, some terrible news reached us. In the middle of their journey, many of them had contracted the horrible vomiting disease known as cholera, and as a result many had died. We were informed that as those remaining were in a terrible state, a rescue mission was being undertaken.

A day or two after this news, we were hurriedly called to the shores of Mullaitivu well past midnight one day. When some of the other female cadres and I arrived there, the Sea Tigers handed over the dead and dying who remained from Commander Keeran's team which had set out for Batticaloa. They were loaded onto waiting vehicles that had already been prepared for them and taken away. I heard that Nirojini, a fighter who was well-known to me, had died of the cholera and been buried in a jungle path. Another fighter, Sutharsini lay there with her eyes closed, looking lifeless like a corpse. The rest were in the same condition. Keeran, who had clung waveringly to his life until then, died the moment they reached the Mullaitivu shore. A separate site had been set up to provide medical care for those most affected. Through intensive care, they were able to recover completely after more than a month. However, it took them several more months to return to good health.

It was only after they recovered that we tried to discover how they had contracted the disease. On their journey they had had a clash with an army troop and were forced to take cover for several days. Their food supplies had run out, and they were forced to eat the dried buffalo meat stores the previous troop had left behind, and drink water from jungle pools; soon after they had been overcome with vomiting and diarrhea. The survivors of that troop told us about their horrifying experiences. As their companions died one by one around them, they were only able to bury a few. They were all wasting away with the disease and had to abandon the bodies of the dead in the forest and escape. All the fighters who heard this story thought it must have been a terrifying experience.

A few months later, the vomiting disease of cholera began to appear among the people of Vanni as well. The medics became alert as soon as they noticed one or two cases showing symptoms of the disease. At a time when they struggled, caught between the hazards of a raging war on the one hand, and poverty and malnutrition on the other, to have a terrifying, infectious, life-threatening disease like cholera spread among them meant unimaginable havoc.

Under the Leader's instructions, the Political Wing worked frantically side by side with the medics. We took up work raising awareness about the disease and caring for the infected. We split up into several teams and worked around the clock, barely closing our eyes. Facts and warning signs of cholera were explained over loudspeakers, in the Eelanatham newspapers, on the Tigers' Voice radio and in special flyers to get the information out to the people promptly. The people cooperated fully in our prevention measures. The villagers themselves brought people showing cholera symptoms to the medical facilities prepared for them.

Bouts of malaria kept continuously breaking out among the people at Vanni as well. The people and the fighters were terribly affected by this. Even hearing the names of those medications, 'Chloroquine, Primaquine, Theraprim' would make me feel nauseous. The malaria I seemed to catch once every six months caused me a great deal of physical suffering as well. Because the medical division continuously kept using the malaria prevention medication, eventually malaria was eradicated in Vanni.

On 13 August 1998, I went to the Kilinochchi area to meet frontline Commander Theepan to gather some data for a frontline article I was writing for 'Freedom Birds'. His command centre was set up in the Thiruvaiyaru area near the battlefield. I knew that there had been a clash with the army in the Konavil area on the first night. However, I did not know too many facts about it. A friend of mine who was at the medical centre nearby came running up to me, held on to my hand and said the words that burned into my soul. 'Thamizhini, our Santhiya was injured in the head at the fighting in Konavil in the Kilinochchi area, and died last night,' she said. While I had always known that in this terrible unending war, either my sister, or I, or both, might die, the news that my sister, who had followed me into the Movement out of her immeasurable love for me, had lost her life in the field before me, tore at my heart.

She was born on 9 July, my sister Nageswari (Gowri) Subramaniam. She studied at the same school I did. Having joined the Movement in 1992, she received combat training with me in the same camp and was taken into the Leopard Brigade. People who saw her fair-skinned, delicate, beautiful appearance would ask in surprise: 'Is this really your sister?' Of the family, she had the most affectionate, mischievous nature, brimming with courage. She would write poetry in her beautiful script and she would draw pictures. At one point in 1997, my sister and I had both got three days leave to go home. The two of us, who had fought often as children fought then as well. Unlike me, spending all my time with my head in a book, she would help my mother with all the housework. She would visit all the relatives. 'I'll soon be joining appa. You take good care of amma,' she kept saying. As usual, I gave her two punches and scolded her, 'Stop talking nonsense like a lunatic.'

At that time, my mother and siblings lived on a property we had in a village called Ilankopuram, in the Viswamadu district. The family lived in poverty. My third younger sister got married. My younger brother had given up his schooling and was working in a shop. The other sisters were in school. Amma had planted a small garden around the house. The loss of my sister had plunged the family into a deep depression. As the war raged on, amma was very afraid that something would happen to me as well. As I prepared to leave immediately after my sister's last rites, my mother hugged me, wailing: 'This is enough; leave the Movement and come home, amma.' I had many responsibilities given to me by the Movement. And many fighters I cared deeply about had already lost their lives. I didn't have the courage to look at my mother's face at that time. I silently drew her hands away from me, and with my head bowed, carrying a heavy burden in my heart, I reached my base.

In 1997–98, the Tigers undertook more than two major attempts to capture Kilinochchi. Many hundreds of cadres, including Black Tigers had lost their lives in these attempts. The third time, in September of 1998, they captured Kilinochchi in Operation 'Unceasing Waves – 02'. This battle went on for three days straight. The places captured by the Tigers on the first day were recaptured by the army on the second day. Apparently, at that time, the Leader had given Thamilselvan, who was at the main command centre, an important mission. As for what it was: he was asked to report back on the morale of the commanders involved in the attack. Following the Leader's request, Thamilselvan talked to the attack commanders Balraj, Theepan and Vithusha and found that they held no great hopes of victory in the attack. When Political Wing leader Thamilselvan informed the Leader of this, it seems he lost his temper and slammed his fist on the table, saying 'I'll win this fight and show them!' After this, the Tigers gained Kilinochchi by hammering the army with the new heavy mortar shells the Movement had acquired. Thamilselvan himself told us this story in a gathering, face to face. More than 500 cadres, including female cadres, lost their lives in this fight. The army, which had retreated from Kilinochchi, did not go far, but set up base where the Paranthan Chemical Corporation was situated.

In the middle of 1999, the attack troop of the Women's Political Wing was based in the Pallamadu Sannar area of Mannar district, under the leadership of Lt. Col. Thanikaichelvi. More than 50 cadres lost their lives in an unexpected attack by the army, who had surrounded the area. Lt. Col. Thanikaichelvi lost her life in this operation as well. Her birthplace was Elaalai in Jaffna. She was one of the founding members of the 'Freedom Birds'. She received her combat training in the fourth women's training base in the Manal Aru forest in 1989. She did political work in many places, including Jaffna and Vanni, became head of the Women's Political Wing, then led the troops travelling to Jaffna, and finally served as head of the Political Wing's attack unit. After we lost her, Lt. Col. Thaarani was appointed to the post of head of the attack unit. I was appointed to continue the work she had been doing as the head of the Women's Political Wing.

In addition to linking up the many women's administrative divisions that functioned under the Political Wing, and running them, it was necessary to also take up many projects for the women in the community. I dreamt of a re-flowering of education and economic growth to help their lives reach great heights. But our main tasks were limited to dealing with administrative problems and recruiting personnel.

After this, on 2 November 1999, the Tigers united the strongest troops in the Movement to begin Operation 'Unceasing Waves – 03,' the massive counterstrike against the 'Jayasikuru' military forces. The Tiger's troops were sent to the lines in Muthayankattu, Samankulam, Mulliyavalai, Thanneeruttru, Katpurapulveli, Kodalikkal and Itthimadu. The aim was to break through the Oddusuddan area that had been captured by the army in a 'watershed' operation, and then advance. The Sri Lankan Navy was stationed there. The Tigers had captured even more areas than they had originally planned to. The main cause for this was the power and shelling range of the 122mm artillery cannons. Due to the attacks that began on 2 November in Katsilaimadu in

Oddusuddan, by 7 November the Tigers successfully captured the stretch of terrain from Omanthai to Neeravi.

The Tigers announced that in the military operation 'Jayasikuru' that had begun in May of 1997 and ended in November 1999 alone, 1,500 fighters and 3,000 army personnel had lost their lives. At the same time, the Sri Lankan army announced that 1,350 had lost their lives in their ranks and 4,000 were injured, while 3,614 of the Tigers' ranks had been killed and 1,899 injured. In sum total, the children of poverty-stricken mothers in the nation of Sri Lanka lost their lives by the thousands on the A9 road and the forests of Vanni, in a battle that did not benefit anyone.

In this period, leader Prabhakaran had created many new troops. However, at that time the children of the Tamil people in Vanni were unable to meet the personnel demands of those troops. After 'Unceasing Waves', the assault brigades were given a period of respite. Malathi Brigade fighters had three days of special leave by the Alampil beach. Those were leisurely days with arrangements for good food, cultural events and sea bathing. The Leader came by daily and would spend time talking to the fighters. I was there with Brigadier Vithusha those days. The Leader also gave special awards to the fighters who had performed exceptionally well in the previous clashes. He gave the female fighters who had attacked and destroyed a tank with the help of an RPG his own telescope as a special prize. None of us knew that this respite was in preparation for another massive strike in the next phase.

On 26 March 2000, the Kudaarappu landing strike took place. They evaded Elephant Pass, for a box-shaped strike in the Ithaavil area carried out under the strategic leadership of Brigadier Balraj. The strike had Malathi Brigade covering Elephant Pass and Major Sothiya brigade covering Chavakachcheri, while Charles Antony Brigade set up some stations as well. The aim was to stop supplies from being transported from Jaffna to Elephant Pass through the A9 road. After the Vadamaradchi East Thaalayadi Road was captured, Brigadier Vithusha asked me to come to the Ithaavil area. I went with some of the female cadres past the Elephant Pass lagoon through Kandaavalai Kombadi, and then past the Thondaimanaru lagoon. The Sea Tigers used ordinary Bluestar boats and low horsepower engines to cross these saltwater lagoons.

You were considered fortunate if you managed to cross the Thondaimanaru lagoon. As the Tigers' stations were set up in a condensed space, the army swept the area endlessly with shells. A heavy artillery team was travelling in a boat ahead of us. Tragically, the boat was struck right before our eyes, and the boat and the fighters in it were submerged in flames as I watched in shock. When we reached Brigadier Vithusha's station, having somehow survived, we only found temporary bunkers with sticks over them, and sandbags piled on top. At the same moment I heard her voice on the high frequency walkie talkie, the whole place shook, and the sandbags and sticks flew into the air. The war at the Ithaavil battlefield raged furiously, reminding me of some suspense-filled English action film you might watch at the edge of your seat. When Elephant Pass was captured on 22 April 2000, the Movement's dream of many years was realized. The battles that had taken place on that saltwater lagoon had claimed many thousand lives.

When Elephant Pass was captured, the Movement expected that the road to Jaffna would be opened. With the hope of capturing Jaffna next, there was a major advance undertaken through the Poonakari Sangupiddy bridge road. The Tigers' long-range artillery was once again used to maximum capacity. A shower of shells fell on the tanks stationed in Poonakari and Kalmunai, and the Thenmaradchi army base. The army launched a frightening counter strike as well. The Tigers' attack troops captured Thenmaradchi's Maravanpulavu Road and brought Chavakachcheri under their control as well. The head of the Political Wing had assigned me to an urgent mission. The fighters were to immediately go to the Kaithady home for the elderly, rescue them and take them to Vanni. Male cadres were attached to this mission as well.

I had prepared the fighters and was sending them through the Sangupiddy bridge. The air force strikes were fierce. Unable to ride my motorcycle on the sandy Poonakari road, I kept one foot on the ground and kept pushing it forward. I heard a tractor speeding behind me. When I tried to move aside to give it some room, the wheel refused to budge, and I fell across the street under the motorcycle. I saw the driver of the tractor stand up on his brakes. The front wheel of the tractor, which had gone out of control, went over my left shoulder when it hit me. They loaded my bike and me onto the tractor and dropped me off at the Poonakari base where I lay in its trailer, in agonizing pain, beside the corpses of fallen fighters.

I went to the Kaithady elders' home through Sangupiddy road, with some painkillers, and my arm in bandages. The fighters who had already reached there were busy at work. The place was in such a disgraceful state, you could barely look at it. The elders who couldn't move unassisted lay dead in their beds in several places in that building; many were injured; those who remained were hiding beneath the fireplaces and inside the rooms shaking with fear, urinating and defecating in the same place.

The smell of blood and the rotting stench arising from the corpses hit you in the face. When the clash between the two sides had begun, the people of Chavakachcheri and Kaithadi had dropped everything on the spot and fled towards Valikamam. The caretakers of the home having fled as well, the elderly residents were abandoned. The Tamil Rehabilitation division of the Political Wing transported the elders by boat to Vanni and set them up in the Ashram situated in Anaivilunthan.

Malathi Brigade had stations in a place past Navatkuli, where Ariyalai Road bifurcates. The people had got caught in the clashes of this battle and had been greatly affected by it. Chavakachcheri town was destroyed by the shelling from both sides. Stores were broken, shattered, and their goods lay smashed on the roads. The Liberation Tigers were all so dizzy with victory, we were unable to clearly reflect on the question that arose in the heart, as to why a liberation struggle for the people would cause so much destruction for those very people. Over 25 border patrol fighters had lost their lives in the Chavakachcheri clashes. Since they were all from the same village, and all related to each other, their loss created a lot of anger and frustration among the people. There were incidents where the people got into arguments and fights with the fighters as well.

When we were unable to advance into Jaffna as the Movement had hoped, the brigades retreated to Vanni again.

After 2001, Kilinochchi began to flourish again. The Liberation Tigers also began to move their political and administrative work back to Kilinochchi. But at first the Tigers did not have the same faith in the defence at Kilinochchi, as they had had in the fortifications at Puthukkudiyiruppu. Many of the Movement's military structures, as well as its main headquarters remained in Puthukkudiyiruppu. The headquarters of the Political Wing and the political school were set up in Kilinochchi Paravippanchan area. We also set up the Women's Front centre for operations in the same area.

It became apparent that the initial phase of plans had started within the Movement to begin covert peace talks between the government and the Tigers, with the help of a third-party mediator. However, at that time the Tigers' leadership had hoped to regain control of Jaffna through an attack using their military strength and only then entertain peace talks. At the same time, the Sri Lankan government must have hoped to recapture Elephant Pass and strengthen their defences in Jaffna before initiating peace talks. Therefore, the battlefield at Mukamalai in Jaffna continued to blaze on. Operation Hini Gala, a military operation undertaken by the army began in 2001 was successfully quashed by the Tigers. After this, Kilinochchi town was firmly established as the political capital of the Tigers.

When the A9 road, which had been drenched in the blood of thousands, was opened in 2002, no one could deny that the Tigers were at the height of their military prowess. The failure of the Tigers' leadership strategy to transform this military strength into a political and diplomatic strength would one day lead to the people themselves pushing open the roads and heading out of Mullivaikkal.

2

I Was Born into War

The broad spreading paddy fields, the water channels that snaked between them, the gravel paths, the sheltering portia trees: my birthplace of Paranthan caressed you with its show of beauty. Paranthan was a small village where the great A9 highway met the two important roads, the Poonakari-Mannar road, and the Mullaitivu road. It was the people from Jaffna who came here to do cultivation in 1936 who eventually settled down here permanently. Free of luxuries, they lived a life of simplicity. About five kilometres south of Paranthan is the town of Kilinochchi, and six kilometres north is the Elephant Pass lagoon. In the old days, in order to prevent the smuggling of ivory and lumber, the Portuguese set up a guard there; then the Dutch built a fort here in 1776, which was taken over by the British, and from 1952 on, the Sri Lankan (Ceylonese) police set up a check point there. Paranthan was well known in Sri Lanka as the site of the Elephant Pass salt flats, and the Paranthan Chemical Corporation.

From the early days of the war, Paranthan began to change into a strategically key battle site as well. As a result, the lives of the people in Paranthan were gradually disrupted, and they became like fledglings displaced from their nests. It was at such a time that I was born. My father, Kanthiah Subramaniam, was from Jaffna. My mother, Sinnamma, was born and raised in Paranthan. I was born, the eldest daughter, when my mother was 17. My maternal grandfather, Swaminathan, was an experienced cultivator.

My parents told me that my grandmother, who was a staunch Amman devotee, had named me Sivakami.

As I was born when the Tamil people were being engulfed by war, my childhood was spent absorbing its impacts. My father was a humble man, of a gentle, loving nature. He was also a habitual reader. He would read everything from history and purana (religious) stories, to political doctrines. He would turn the things he read into children's stories and narrate them to me at night. As I was born when my mother was very young, and had several siblings, I was raised mostly in my grandmother's house, as her favourite. The oldest grandchild in our family, I was loved by everyone. My uncle, my mother's only brother, chose to stay home and farm instead of looking for a government job, even though he had completed his A levels. My grandfather's younger brother, Sethupathy, never married, but lived as a member of his brother's family. A tireless worker, and a stern man, he managed the welfare of our large extended family. I am amazed even today at their character and disciplined way of life, even though they were not highly educated. They raised us children as if we were their lives. I had never been punished by my parents or elders or ever heard a harsh word from their mouths.

The sweetest moments in my memory are of travelling in a bullock cart tied to a pair of buffaloes whose bells made a jingling noise as we travelled to Karadipokku Junction to watch films at the Eswaran or Parasakthi theatres. There we would sit as a family on mats set out over straw and watch ammamma's favorite Sivaji or MGR films halfway, and spend the other half curled up sleeping on our elders' laps; we usually arrived home fast asleep.

Their loving guidance gave me a sense of independence even from an early age. Though I was an ordinary girl from a farming family, they never tried to control me, or force their opinions or habits on me. On the contrary, they wanted me to study well and reach a higher level in life. That was their dream as well.

I began my studies at Paranthan's Hindu Maha Vidyalayam and went as far as the Advanced Level. Up to the point where I did my Ordinary Levels, the railway was still operating, and teachers from Jaffna and from our area taught there. There were many teachers in

Thamizhini with her parents and sister

Thamizhini's mother

my school who cared for their students as if they were their own children. They nurtured great ambitions in their students for their future lives. I was determined to study and go on to university. I did not know at the time that the cyclone of war that was germinating in the country would sweep away our modest hopes.

From the time I had any understanding of what was happening around me, the tranquil life of our village was frequently disrupted. It became the norm to hear gunshots on the street every day. The elders would secretly discuss who had fired the gun and who had died. Sometimes these kinds of incidents would happen during a school day. At those times the parents would come by, even in the middle of the day, and take the children home. The teachers would announce that the school was closing and leave as well. The shops were closed, the streets were empty, and we would stay shut in our houses for so many days, not knowing what was going on, fearing for our lives. At an age when we couldn't understand what was happening and why, our tender shoulders bore the heavy burden of this war.

When I was in the sixth grade, I had gone one day to the neighbouring village of Kumarapuram for an afternoon class. My school was situated there as well. Shortly after classes began, loud explosions were heard from the direction of the Paranthan Junction. The teacher stopped the class immediately. Everyone was in shock. Some students began to cry. As soon as the explosions ceased, the teacher asked us all to run home as fast as we could. When I got home, frightened and in tears, I discovered that the sounds of the explosion had reached the front yard of our house. The neighbours had gathered in our front yard reeling from the shock. Our house was beside the A9 road. Two young men belonging to some group had been putting up posters on the walls in front of our house, when some military personnel who had been doing their rounds in civilian clothing, began shooting at them at random. When this happened, the young men had jumped the wall and begun running toward our house. One youth was shot in the head right in front of our house and died then and there. The other youth ran to the back and escaped by way of the railway track that ran behind our house. While this was happening, ammamma had been winnowing rice on the verandah. She walked about in a daze for a few days, from the shock brought on by this unexpected incident; it frightened us to see her this way. She told us that a living boy had died twitching in front of her, and that the body had been dragged away by the army.

It was customary for the Movement's representatives to organize gatherings for the senior students at my school. They would not include children from my grade in those gatherings. They would dismiss us and chase us away saying that we were only going to be noisy. But we were so curious to find out what was going on there that we would hang on the low walls and peer in, without going home. Every day, different annas with new and different names would come by to organize a gathering. They would speak with great anger and passion. The annas and akkas in our school would ask them questions. Some days there would be heated debates. Even if we didn't understand all of it, the weapons they carried, and their serious faces left a deep impression on us.

In the times following, many of the older students from our school kept disappearing. The students whispered among themselves in the classrooms: 'These ones went to train with this Movement, the other ones went to train with that Movement.' Sometimes

Thamizhini as a child

relatives would gather at the homes of the youth who had left for the Movements from our village, and lament loudly, as if they were at a funeral.

It became the norm to put up posters for Movement groups on the tall water tank at our school. The students who were divided in their support for different factions became so competitive that close friends fell out over this. They were often engaged in arguments and fights.

When some of the youth who had gone for training returned to the village, they would be completely altered in appearance. They were so highly esteemed in the community that even the village elders treated them with respect. They would advise students like us in the lower grades, saying, 'We're going to fight so that you can study well and advance in life.' The young boys and girls hero-worshipped the youth who walked around with their weapons more than any film stars. Seeing them and being friendly with them elevated you in the eyes of others as well. They too behaved like family, referring to everyone as either 'amma, appa, thambi or thangachi' and mingling with ease.

The Kilinochchi police station had been transformed into a military camp. It must have been 1986. One day, that camp was attacked by one of the groups around midnight. The fire burned bright as the afternoon sun in the middle of the night and could be seen as far away as Paranthan. The villages surrounding Kilinochchi were startled out of their sleep. A helicopter circled overhead, firing occasionally. Paying no attention to the stalks that tore at our legs in the harvested fields, families fled together in the dead of the night.

The Sri Lankan army continued to strengthen their base in the Kilinochchi area. The Movements' fighters launched counter-strikes against the soldiers coming out of there. At this time, our family, who lived so close to the A9, suffered untold misery. Every time we heard the news that the army was coming, we dropped everything as it was and ran through the paths in the paddy fields. We would only return home in the evenings, when the sound of explosions had stopped. Until then, the elders struggled to staunch the children's hunger. Often, we'd be running with our schoolbags in hand. Our sinnathaatha would carry whatever food was available and go with us. I was at an age where I could understand a few things, and I hated losing our peace and having to run around like this.

The army began launching shells in the direction of Paranthan from Kilinochchi. One afternoon, sinnathaatha went to put out water for the bullocks that had been tied up for grazing in the morning. Suddenly we heard the crash of shells landing near where he was. There was a cloud of smoke. When the rest of the house ran out screaming, they saw him hobbling back, holding his shawl to his stomach. A piece of shrapnel had torn through his stomach. Part of his intestine had come out through the wound. Even though my uncle had his own car, we could not drive him to the hospital, because an air-force helicopter kept circling the Paranthan area and attacking continuously. That day I cried with anger and frustration. I was shaking with the fear that we might not be able to save our thaatha. I was resolved that if such a thing happened, I would immediately enlist in the Movement. A little while later, when the helicopters had left the area, we were able to get him to the hospital and save his life. After losing my father in an accident, it was my uncle and maternal grandparents who had raised us. We had such great love for them.

There were now frequent clashes between the Movements and the army in Paranthan Junction. On top of this, the Movements also clashed with each other. I could not understand why the annas who so clearly explained the need to fight against the army in all those gatherings were now warring amongst themselves. The things I saw, because I had to pass by the Paranthan Junction to get to school every day, made me lose hope that a peaceful future lay ahead for us. Instead it paved the way for deeper fear and anxiety.

It was during this time that the Indian Forces arrived. I was in the tenth grade at the time. The elders said among themselves that this would be the answer to all our problems. Like everyone else, we too stood in the streets and waved our welcome to the Indian Peace Keeping Forces.

The Indian Forces set up a massive base on the site of the Northern Region Grain Research Centre, between Paranthan and Karadipokku, taking up the huge storehouses as well as the researchers' quarters. They spoke many languages that we had never heard until then. The long-haired, bearded Punjabis, and the turmeric-skinned short-statured Gurkhas paraded the India we only knew from schoolbooks before our eyes. Our tuition centre, 'Science Centre', was situated in Karadipokku. The students from Kumarapuram and Paranthan would go there in crowds. As soon as they saw the girls, the Indian soldiers would shout out: 'Hey kutti, hey kutti, shall we "get married"?' and other obscene things in several different languages. We were so terrified of them we couldn't even turn our heads.

In this way the brief time of peace we had was disrupted again. The people said the Liberation Tigers' Movement had begun a war with the Indian Forces. It had become a dangerous time for young women. Word began to spread that the Indian Forces has sexually assaulted young women in some areas in Jaffna. I did not know if such incidents had also happened in Kilinochchi. Periyappa brought his daughter to our house and left her there night after night because they feared it wasn't safe to keep akka in their home. It was quite the struggle for our grandparents to take care of us young women, and to send us to school and for tuition classes. At that time, I was preparing for my GCE Ordinary Levels exam.

One day, during school hours, we were frightened by the sounds of heavy gunfire. The whole town of Paranthan was surrounded. We students huddled under our desks in fear. Shortly after, the Indian Forces who had entered our school grounds poured into every classroom. They asked our principal some questions and began beating him. When we saw our revered principal being beaten where he stood, in front of us, his lip swollen and bleeding, the students began crying out loud. Then the people of the town, men and women, were brought into the school playground with their hands above their heads and made to kneel on the ground. Their task of searching for the Tigers who had escaped after attacking them stretched out into the evening.

Going to school and afternoon tuition every day was like walking on fire. We heard that some Tamil youth who were collaborating with the Indian Forces were forcibly taking away young men for training. As a result, many young men in our classes stopped their studies and went missing. The Tamil youth with red cloth tied around their heads would stand with the Indian Forces almost the length of the road. When we saw their leers and heard their taunts, we felt a frustration and fury bubbling over inside us. We schoolchildren had no choice but to bear it. We felt boundless respect and faith in the members of the Liberation Tigers Movement, who hid in the forest and carried out their attacks. We began to dream that only they could bring an end to these unending miseries.

As far as I am concerned, I had few memories of enjoying the sweetness or joys of my teenage years. Going to the Kumarapuram Murugan temple festival in June, in my pavadai thavani (long skirt and blouse), with my classmates, and hearing the nathaswaram player playing the hit song 'Rasathi manasila', and giggling to ourselves dreaming that he was looking at us when he played; going to a Santhan concert at the Porikadalai Amman temple and falling asleep in the afternoon maths tuition class the next day, and having the tuition teacher scold us, 'You listen to Santhan singing about the waning moon and wear yourselves out till dawn, and then come here to sleep' and make us all stand outside the class; sharing my own opinions of Kamal Hasan and Rajnikanth films with my friends; all these still linger in my memory.

When Premadasa and the Tigers agreed to a ceasefire in 1990, once again the elders said our problems would finally be over. But the youth in our classes secretly averred among themselves that if the troubles returned, joining the Tigers would be their best option. I, on the other hand, though I had a great desire to do something for my people, did not think of joining the Movement to fight. My ambition was to go to university and further my education. I was the secretary of the Student Council, and a school prefect. I had been involved in public speaking, poetry, debate teams, drama and all manner of activities since I was very young, and not only received praise from the officials and teachers in my school but was known at other schools as well. There was no room in my mind for anything other than to go to university, get a good job and financially support my fatherless family.

In the 1990s, in a time when peace was taking hold, the Tigers' Movement grew in the land. I heard that many male students who were in school with me had joined the Movement. One or two female students had gone missing as well. Stories spread among the people that women had already joined the Movement and were active within it. I knew about the 'Freedom Birds', the women's group that had existed from the time of Thileepan, who died during his hunger strike in Jaffna. But it was only during the nineties that we saw them in person; the women in camouflage uniform, carrying weapons. Though the community disparaged the women who joined the Movement in the early days, as time went on, they eventually came to accept the female fighters and got used to them. The girls in the village in Paranthan began to visit people in their homes and interact with them. I too was awed by their unusually courageous way of life, though they seemed like ordinary women just like us. I wanted very much to be friends with them. One day, when I went to their camp with some of my friends from school, I was surprised to see my younger sister there already. We had both been caught in the act we had tried to keep secret from our family. We promised each other not to breathe a word of this at home.

There were frequent gatherings of the Tigers' student groups in our school. The founding principle for the student organization was that it wasn't necessary for you to join the Movement to fight. You could also provide support for the struggle by staying in the student group and continuing your studies. I was chosen to be the leader of the student organization in my school. It was at this juncture that the peace talks between the Tigers and the Premadasa government began to rupture. Many events were organized to galvanize the people, and to rally the students. The students from my school also participated with great fervour and shouted slogans. Slogans like, 'Student strength is a powerful strength', 'Don't force the hand that raises a pen to raise a gun', raised our feelings to a fever pitch. As student group representatives, we participated in all the public meetings and rallies.

At the end of the 1990s, the war between the Tigers and the Sri Lankan Armed Forces exploded. Their successful attacks, including the destruction of the army camps in Kokavil and Mankulam, and the raising of the Tiger flag at the Jaffna Fort, created a great wave of support for the Tigers from the community. The fighters were praised as victorious heroes. The rebel songs released at the time, 'This soil is our own soil', 'We go in search of the enemy hideout' and others like them, roused the feelings of the young men and women. They joined the Movement in thousands upon thousands. The 1991 GCE A' Levels were indefinitely postponed. In July of that year, the Tigers began a joint aerial and ocean attack on the army camp at Elephant Pass. The people of Paranthan, including my family, were all displaced, and we moved to Tharmapuram.

The Tigers were able to undertake some rearguard work through the student groups. A variety of tasks were given over to the students: gathering dry rations from the people, caring for the injured and making floral garlands for the dead fighters who could not be returned to their families. At the time I was leading the school band. Our instrumental band was taken to play funeral music for the memorial services for the dead Tigers. Ordinarily, Tamil women aren't allowed in the graveyard, but we went to the graves of the fallen. All fighters present would light the pyre for the dead warriors from the outer districts. That sight melted my heart. It gave rise to a tremendous sense of guilt, that I was a mere spectator in a time when hundreds of young men and women were giving up their lives every day. I didn't think that I'd be able to resume further studies any time soon. The sights I saw day and night tormented me. I came to believe that if at least one person in every family went to fight, the other siblings could live in peace. I decided that I should go, rather than see my younger siblings go off to fight and face a death like this. I didn't consider asking anyone's advice on the matter.

It was an agony to be parted from my mother and siblings. I was convinced that I would never see them again in my life. I lied to my mother, saying that I was going for my afternoon lessons, and took my bicycle and set off. I went to the female fighters' camp in Kilinochchi's Kanagapuram and asked to enlist in the Movement. There were more than a hundred women like me who had already joined up, sitting under the mango trees there. They were ready to be shipped off for training to Jaffna, through the Poonakari Sangupiddy route. I removed the earrings and watch I was wearing and gave them to the official there. They said they would give them back to amma. I also wrote amma a short letter, handed it over to them, and went to join the troop of recruits. I enlisted in the Liberation Tigers' Movement as a fighter on 29 July 1991. At that time, and under those circumstances, I did not see myself as having any other choice. I truly believed I had made the right decision with my life. Our senior political leaders proclaimed war from their platforms, and the younger generations' lives were made sacrificial offerings in the funeral pyre of war. Thousands of young people were eagerly heading towards those flames.

3

The Political Cadre Undergoes Combat Training

I was told that my maama, amma and thaatha had come in search of me, and were waiting at the entrance to the Kanakapuram women's training camp. They had somehow discovered that I had joined the Movement, rather than go home as usual after my afternoon classes. The akka in charge called me, saying: 'Go, speak to them and come.' I didn't go. I was afraid to face them, because I thought they would dull the heat of my determination with their affection and take me back home. I asked the akka in charge to give them the letter I had written for them. I didn't have the courage to look at their faces or see the tears of those loving gods who had borne me on their shoulders and in their arms. I went off and sobbed and sobbed all alone. I had never been away from my family even for a day since the day I was born. I felt a panic at the thought of being separated so abruptly and completely from them. I suppressed my grief, and steeled myself, because it was foremost in my mind that everyone here had left their families and come here for the sake of the nation, just like me.

The next night the head of the Women's Political Wing of the Vanni district came to meet us. 'The Movement is struggle, struggle is the Movement,' she began, and she spoke to us new recruits for a long time. 'From now on, the Movement is your family, the people here are your relatives. The Leader is our mother, father, everything. The foremost duty of a fighter in the Movement is to follow orders.'

She explained some of the fundamentals for us. After that, we were given Movement names in place of our own. The name I was given at that time was Chandrika. We were told that from that moment on, we could not use our own names; if we used them

Thamizhini with family members

by mistake, we would be punished. We had been informed that Lt. Col. Chandran, who had been the Political Aide in Vanni District, had been injured in a battle with the army, and died as he was being transported by boat to Tamil Nadu for surgery. As he was a relative on my mother's side, the chief told me that I had been named after him.

More than 200 recruits had enlisted there. The new recruits kept joining up. So, there was a hubbub as arrangements were made to send them to the training bases in Jaffna immediately. As the battle at Elephant Pass continued, helicopters kept circling overhead and firing intermittently. We were shut up in I-shaped bunkers in the mango tree groves near the Kanakapuram base for whole days. Of that group, 12 of us were selected and separated from the rest. The chief met with us privately and said: 'You have been selected for political work. We can't each do whatever we wish in the Movement. We must take up the work the Movement chooses for us. So, you won't be sent out with this troop. I'll tell you what you need to do, later.' After that, we were kept separate from the others. The minibuses arrived, to transport everyone to the women's training base in Jaffna. I felt cheated that I couldn't go with the rest of them to the training base, but I kept quiet and didn't show my disappointment. The next day we were given new uniforms. When I wore my uniform and shoes for the first time, I felt a courage and pride seep into me. We were loaded into a pickup and taken to a base set up in the forest area of Mankulam. We were kept there for about a month and given some basic training. Along with loading and unloading weapons, running and physical training, we were taught how to interact with civilians, the history of the Movement, and the histories of the Heroes. None of this training was at all difficult for me. In the beginning, waking up at four in the morning, going to sleep after ten at night, and the night watch duties at midnight were tough. After this training, we were sent out to different districts with senior members who had already done political work there. I was sent to the village of Makilankulam in the Vavuniya district.

At that time, the village was a simple habitation surrounded by dense forest. We went door to door and met with the people. We enquired about the conditions of women and children. My job was basically going 'double' on a bicycle and writing my notes in a copybook. The akka who had charge of me already knew many of the people there. It gave me great joy to get to know the people like this. A new village, new faces. I saw the faces of my family in the faces of those humble people who welcomed us. There was a middle-aged mother in our base. She had lost her two sons in the struggle. She was very loving towards the fighters who worked in the primary health centre there. She would take on any difficult task without tiring. None of our fighters could cycle as fast as she could. At night, as we lay down to sleep, we would ask: 'Aunty, sing us a song?' She would start singing songs she had written herself, tapping out the rhythm as she sang beautifully: 'At a school-going age, he joined a troop, at a wandering, playful age, he picked up the gun....' That mother, who had suffered so much grief in her life, became a fighter herself. Of the many women personalities I met, she holds a special place in my heart.

No matter how well we performed, we were not considered or valued as full members of the Movement because we had not received traditional basic weapons training. When you were introduced to a member of the Movement, the first question they asked you was: 'What was your training base number?' When we were forced to reply: 'We haven't had combat training yet', we would be looked upon as inferiors. It was hard to bear. We would think to ourselves that it was, after all, the Movement that was preventing us from going for training. It was the nighttime that I found especially hard. We had to take individual turns to keep watch, and often my turn seemed to come at around midnight. I had to stand prepared to fire a weapon I hadn't been trained to use. Even as a child I had never been afraid of ghosts, but the spread of trees in the forest, the all-engulfing darkness, the buzz of insects, the sudden, eerie sounds of birds and animals, and the sense of isolation filled me with a dread in the pit of my stomach like nothing I had known. At those times, I was haunted by memories of the stories of demons and ghosts my grandmother used to tell me when I was a child. I would run through all the Thevaram and Thiruvasakam chants I knew in my mind. But I would never show my fear on my face, or in my actions. It was a matter of pride for me, partly because I was afraid that if I showed my fear, they would not send me for combat training. It wasn't just me, all the cadres there felt the same.

Every Friday, I had to take someone 'double' on the bicycle from Makilankulam in Vavuniya, to Mankulam, to pick up the programme reports. I had to cycle along the bumpy sand paths, with a gun slung over my shoulder, watching out for soldiers hiding in the thick forests on either side, to get onto the A9 in the Omanthai area to take it to Mankulam, and then take the side roads to return to the site where the base was located. Though it was hard at first, to cycle the distance of all these kilometres, I became used to it after a while.

After three months had passed in this way, another cadre and I were informed that we had been selected to be sent to the Liberation Tigers' headquarters for the women's vanguard in Thinnaveli. Perhaps out of the captain's faith in our skills, he sent us off by ourselves with just the address. When I used to live at home, I went to Jaffna with the elders. I knew the Jaffna bus depot, Nallur Murugan temple, the ice cream shop and Malayan Café. I didn't know any other places, really. All travel to Jaffna went through the Poonakari-Sangupiddy route. Somehow, we got past Sangupiddy road and through Maravanpulavu road to Chavakachcheri Junction. The cadre who came with me was from Tharmapuram. Her father was a school principal, and her mother a teacher. As we stood there, when we got to Jaffna, not sure how to get to Thinnaveli, we plucked up the courage to raise our hands and stop a vehicle that was passing us. Luckily, there were other cadres in the vehicle. With a sense of relief, we said: 'Anna, we need to get to the Political base in Thinnaveli.' 'Oh, you're the kids doing the political work, are you? Come on.' And they picked us up. Those male cadres took us all the way into the compound of the base and dropped us off.

The base covered a large area. There were many high-ranking members of the Liberation Tigers' Women's Front there. Some came in and out for meetings. They were always furiously working. The captain, who came to welcome us, the new recruits from Vanni, heard all our details and explained some of the basics. After she had sent off the cadre who accompanied me to another base, she gave me the task of compiling reports in her office. Someone else explained how I was expected to write those out. I was told those reports were to be sent to Mahattaya, the deputy leader of the Movement, and the head of the People's Front of the Liberation Tigers.

As secretary to the senior in charge of reports, an endless number of tasks were heaped on me. Compiling and writing out the reports that were sent from each municipality at the end of every month was no easy labour. All the reports had to be read carefully, and the news about the projects undertaken in each area had to be compiled under general categories. As a result of the work I was given, I was able to learn a lot about the projects undertaken by the Movement's Women's Political wing, and the administrative problems related to them.

The head of our Women's Front added me to the list of combatant speakers for the gatherings organized by the Jaffna district political wing. I was given the additional task of going at the appointed times and participating in the gatherings listed on the schedule they gave me. As a result, I got to go to different areas, like Vadamaradchi, Thenmaradchi and Valikamam. Though I had not received basic training, they had me speaking on a wide range of subjects among the higher commissars, brigadiers and senior members of the Movement, all of whom had had long-term experience in and knowledge of the activities of the Movement. Though I spoke with great fear and trembling, I learned to prepare my words appropriately for the gathering. When I had the opportunity, I would go to the injured senior members and eagerly listen to their stories. I searched out the books and newspapers released by the Tigers and read them all very carefully. At such a gathering, after hearing my speech, Mahattaya anna applauded loudly, praising me by saying that this was how a Movement speech should sound. In addition to earning the praise of many other senior fighters, I was unswerving in my attempts to speak to the people in a way that was appropriate for them, and easy for them to understand. On another occasion, the leadership entrusted me with the task of speaking on behalf of the Liberation Tigers' Movement before tens of thousands of people at a Pongu Thamizh Vizha (Rise Tamil Festival).

Though I was working as a secretary at the Women's Front headquarters, in charge of the progress reports, and speaking at these public events, I always felt inferior. The reason being that I had not been sent for basic combat training, which was the foundation for any fighter. There were many like me, in the political wing, who hadn't received combat training. There were about 20 of us in my base alone. Suddenly one day, the base was made ready to welcome an important member. We were all given new white shirts, long black trousers and new shoes and the task of serving tea and refreshments to the people attending the meeting. We got ourselves appropriately prepared and waited. We didn't have any other information. In the Movement, it was considered an infraction to seek information beyond what you were given.

A little while later, a Pajero drove up. Brigadier Sornam and a few others got out of it. After they had looked over the arrangements for the meeting, and the surrounding area, they circled the base and stood guard. Following that, another vehicle pulled up. The Leader of the Movement, Hon. Prabhakaran and his aides got out. When we saw him come out, a majestic smile on his face, we were struck speechless, and hid and watched him. We already knew of him through newspapers and books; we had heard many stories about him from the senior fighters, after we joined the Movement; but I had never even dreamed that I would see the Leader this close, in person.

It was at the battle of Elephant Pass that the female cadres had participated in the fighting in large numbers for the first time. In the month-long battle, many fighters had lost their lives; many others were seriously wounded and had lost limbs. The Leader had come specially to meet the amputees among the female cadres. We began to serve the visitors tea and refreshments. The injured women fighters were overjoyed to speak to the Leader and laughed as they spoke to him. I was amazed that they didn't seem to feel the same kind of fear with him as they did with their own commissars and brigadiers. With a sort of familial entitlement with which they might speak to their mother or father, they called him 'anna, anna' and voiced all their problems to him. It became clear from the conversations that happened there, and the projects that were undertaken shortly after, that the Leader's intention in that meeting was to get the women amputees involved in work that was more accessible for them. As the Leader got ready to leave, he suddenly called out to our commissar and asked: 'Bring the other children for a while,' and all of us who had watched him covertly were brought face to face with him. When we saw the joy on his face, our faith in the Movement was strengthened. He asked each of us our names. As he realized some of us had English sounding names, he said to the commissar: 'Shouldn't these children be given meaningful Tamil names? Look, great heroes with names like Miller, Tempo, Borg. One day they'll start researching which countries they might have come from to fight here.' Then he asked us about the work we were given. 'What else is there? Tell me,' he said. With no hesitation, we said in one voice, 'Anna, send us for combat training.' 'Oho… they're hiding you all away here without sending you for training, is it?' he smiled. 'We can't send you all in one troop for training. The work will be affected. I'll arrange for you to be sent in groups of 10 to different training bases,' he said as he bid us goodbye.

Our commissar called me one day: 'I'm going to put you in charge of a village project. There will only be one other cadre with you,' he said as he explained the work. I was sent to the village with my belongings the very same day. Like a small bird with a palm fruit hoisted on its head, within a few months of joining the Movement I began to be anxious and afraid with all the work I had been entrusted with. My mind was obsessed with getting everything right.

A brush factory had been set up beside the Kilali beach, in the name of the Great Hero Chandranayaki. They had to gather husk from the coconut fields and bury it in sea sand for up to six months. After that, it would be beaten to separate the fibres, and the fibres would be used for making rope, brooms and other household items. The aim with this project was to provide work opportunities for the women of that village. In addition, I had to do the Movement's project reports for the village as well. This kind of project seemed especially daunting in the beginning, for someone as inexperienced as I was. But as I consulted with the more experienced elders of the village, and completed the tasks one by one, my self-confidence and enthusiasm grew as well. About 10 women from the village worked on that project. Though it was only able to garner them about 3000 rupees a month in income, in those circumstances that project was a huge help to them.

We set up a women's organization in that village and put it in charge of a primary school and primary health care centre we created. In that village, two women cadres, without any help from the male cadres, managed to complete these projects with the wholehearted help of the people alone.

At that time, some female troops of the Liberation Tigers were based along the Kilali shore, with the intention of frustrating the military based in Elephant Pass or Poonakari, should they attempt any manoeuvres to advance into Jaffna through Kilali. Brigadier Vithusha was in charge of the troop of 150 fighters. Vithusha must have been amazed by the fact that two new recruits, who hadn't received any combat training, were working so furiously in the village, and that we had such a close relationship with the villagers. She would often call us over in the afternoons, to talk to us. She had us join in the firearms training with her troop, as they practised on the shore. She showed us, neglected political cadres, tremendous care and concern. When I caught cerebral malaria that was spreading like a fury at that time, she had me hospitalized immediately, and showed great concern for my well being, until I returned to good health after convalescing for more than a month.

After this, I was transferred out of Kilali. I was among the cadres selected to study legal administration. At that time, the special Brigadier of the Women's Front met with us. 'Anna has asked that the young people who did not receive basic combat training be sent for training in small groups. So, these young people need to be sent first,' she said. Arrangements were made for 52 of the female cadres who were engaged in political work to join the troop that was being formed at Sothiya base in Kilali for training.

Around April in 1992, I was sent to the Sothiya training base to receive training in the 21st Battalion. I found that my sister was also there for training. She told me story after story of the sadness my family felt at my leaving. She cried, asking me to leave the

Movement, that she would remain to take my place. I reprimanded her. How many thousands were fighters like us? I explained that it was better to fight and die for the people, than to die pointlessly. The CO and the trainers there all knew that she and I were sisters. So, I pointed it out to her that our talking together like this, and spending time together was against regulations. My sister also understood that we should not be insensitive to the feelings of other fighters who, like us, had to leave their families behind. After that, during our training period, I avoided speaking to my sister, or seeing her. I was determined not to see her struggling during the rigorous training or being penalized by the instructors. My sister excelled in combat training and all other tasks and became the Leader of the training team.

There were around 250 people who trained in our base. There were fighters from every district. There were some very young ones too. Though our combat trainers were very tough on the field, they showed great care and compassion for each fighter's individual situation.

The running and physical training that began at 6 am in the morning, only ended at nine. After that, we had an hour to stand in a long line and get our breakfast and tea. Then we had weapons training from 10 am to noon. After that, from noon to one in the afternoon, we had self-defence exercises in the hot sun, on burning sand. With sweat pouring in rivers, we had to stand our ground with our weapons. The SLR used by the Indian army was extremely long. It was our training weapon. The unending training, day and night exhausted the fighters. We got to rest on Sundays, cultural events were held at night. An akka from the 1st battalion of the Women's Front was our main instructor. There was not as much beating of recruits or excessive penalties in our base, as there were in other bases. Contrary to that, she spent a lot of time with the trainees. She conducted herself in a way that instilled fear in those who saw her, but she kept the fighters under tight rein through her own unique approach. She had a distinctive personality for guiding others.

After the three months of training were done, we were sent for further rearguard training for the battlefield. The female cadres were based in sections of Ariyalai, in Jaffna. I was sent as the person in charge of a team of 50 cadres to set up trenches for lengthy manoeuvres, as well as basic bunkers. While we were working there, for some reason, we were not sent food for two days. The fighters, who had been active in the arduous work of digging bunkers, were weak and exhausted. It was the time when palmyrah fruit were ripening and falling from the trees, so they searched for a windfall in the nearby properties and began sucking on the palm fruits they found. On the afternoon of the second day, some food arrived in a small bucket. The fighters, unable to bear their hunger, began to cry when they saw the size of the bucket. The food in it was barely enough for 10 people. We mixed all the food together and each ate just one handful of rice.

After completing six whole months of training, I was sent back to do political work. My sister was sent to the Leopard Brigade. After that, I didn't have the opportunity to see my sister again for another three years. When I heard news of my fellow trainees' heroes' deaths in the battlefront, I was tormented by the guilt that I too should have gone to the battlefield with them. The Political cadres were split up at Jaffna headquarters and sent on different missions. The CO called me aside and sent me to take charge of an agricultural farm.

The Tigers established a judiciary division in 1991. But they had not set up courts. The police had not expanded their role either. During this time, any crimes that occurred in the community were investigated and judged by the governing officers of the area. These farms had been set up primarily for the detention of women who had been punished for their involvement in criminal activity. The large Muskan Farm complex set up in Punnalaikkadduvan was established as a rehabilitation farm for women and was run by the Liberation Tigers' Women's Front. I was put in charge of this complex. There were approximately 30 women detained there, charged with various crimes by the Liberation Tigers.

These women were sent here as prisoners after they had been charged with a crime by the district officers and investigated and sentenced by a member of the judiciary division. They were accused of a variety of crimes like brewing moonshine, theft, infanticide and sex work. They were assigned work in that farm, which had fertile red soil. When I was sent there, I spoke to each of them individually, and openly. I was completely stunned by what I learned: of the secrets kept hidden by our society, and the societal norms that criminalized only women for certain activities. The tearful stories of those women were my first lessons in deepening my understanding of the problems facing women as a whole in our society.

Though the main work in my family was rice cultivation, I knew very little about agricultural farming. I found an elder in the Inuvil area, who had some expertise, and befriended him and asked his advice. He began enthusiastically spending his free time in our garden. He taught the women in our farm what to plant during each season, how to construct proper irrigation trenches and what sort of fertilizers and pesticides to use. The farm flourished and grew so much produce I could hardly believe my eyes. The women seemed to absorb these lessons on agricultural farming very well too. We sold the harvested fruits and vegetables at the Chunnakam market. We had been told that the necessities of the women in that complex had to be managed through our farming income. The accounts had to be shown to the legal division of the Women's Front. That income had to stretch to help the women once they left the farm as well. Once they fulfilled their sentences of three months, or six months, they were sent home with 5000 rupees for living expenses and 25 kilos of dry rations including rice, flour, sugar and lentils.

While these women were living in the complex, they were permitted to visit their families once a month and submit a report to a member of the Women's Front. The needs of the family, especially the needs of the children, had to be brought to the attention of the district officer and fulfilled immediately. At the same time, for three months after these women returned home, we had to analyse the progress they made in their lives and meet their needs. The truth is, the four members who were assigned these tasks had no means to accomplish them, apart from a bicycle they were each given. Even then, it was a huge struggle to cycle on the routes to Vadamaradchi and Thenmaradchi in the heat and against the heavy wind.

During this time, Brigadier Vithusha had taken charge as the second deputy head of the Women's Brigade. She had the authority to make decisions related to the specific issues facing the female fighters and changing organizational responsibilities. When she came to the Punnalaikkaduvan women's correctional farm and saw the projects we had undertaken, she was very surprised, and praised us.

In April of 1993, I was appointed in charge of the Women's Front in Valikamam in Jaffna. Our political base was set up in Oorelu. There were 20 cadres there with me. I was the least experienced member of that group. In the beginning I wondered how I would move anything forward with this crew, but as time passed, I didn't find it to be a difficult task.

THE MAHATTAYA PROBLEM

It was in early 1993 that the accusations of treachery against Mahattaya began to sweep the Movement like a giant wave. Among the senior members, the news created a great sense of shock and distress. Many cried, and some were furious. I had heard from many of the senior women cadres that it was Mahattaya who had been responsible for a very large share of the work in building the foundations of the Movement's growth in Vanni, in the mid 1980s, when the Leader was permanently situated in India. Some of the senior women cadres who had been brought in by him said he was responsible for strategically drawing many women out of other Movements and into the Tigers and having them trained. Our combat trainer had also told us many times that it was Mahattaya anna who had organized many strikes against the Indian Army out of Vanni when the Tigers began to launch attacks on them, and guided the women's brigades that were employed in those strikes.

As a less experienced, junior political cadre at the time, while the Mahattaya affair did not impact me deeply in a personal way, it was still a shock to hear of the corruption of someone who had served as Deputy Head of the Movement. I had only met Mahattaya anna once or twice in person. During a speech training class for the political cadres, in Vadamaraadchi, we had to speak impromptu on a random topic drawn for us. When I finished speaking on the topic I was given, Mahattaya anna smiled, clapped his hands and praised me; that's all I remembered of him.

The public also knew that his camp in Manipay had been surrounded, and that he had been taken into custody by Brigadier Sornam. At that time, something like this happening in the Movement was big news to the people, and it was widely spoken of. 'What happened to Mahattaya?' was the question we faced from the public in every direction. It was a confusing time for junior cadres like us, and we could not make sense of it. The senior fighters explained to us that he had betrayed (Prabhakaran) anna. He had become an agent for the Indian intelligence organization RAW and had plotted to kill the Leader and become the head of the Movement himself.

It was unacceptable for the fighters to discuss the secrets of the Movement, or to pry beyond the tasks we were assigned. The received wisdom was that spilling the secrets of the Movement would result in the speaker receiving a hundred lashes, and the listener receiving 500 lashes. So, the cadres were afraid to gather around to discuss unnecessary matters.

Mahattaya had organized the Political wing of the LTTE according to the framework of a political party. In addition to the Liberation Tigers' People's Front, and the Women's Front, organizations like the Tribunal and Citizen's Committee had been operating among the people as well. It was a time when large photos of the Leader and Mahattaya standing together were prominently displayed in every base. It was habitual in the Movement to refer to some as 'Mahattaya's people'. Even among the female cadres there were some who had boundless faith in Mahattaya anna.

After Mahattaya's arrest, some changes were brought about in the organizations he had established. The Tiger's political wing, which had been called the 'People's Front' up to then, formally became the 'Political Wing'. The Special Brigadier of Jaffna District, Dinesh (Thamilselvan) was appointed as its head. All Mahattaya's political work took on entirely different forms. The 50 or so members of the 'Education Committee' that he had set up were separated and assigned different work. It was a time of 'silent confusion' in the Movement, as waves crashed about in our minds then.

I was in charge of the Women's Front in Valikamam district at the time. I had to meet with the people every day, and often had to speak at meetings as well. The centre of Jaffna was contained in the large area of Valikamam district. Seven circle secretariats had been established below it. Of those areas, designated as Yazh circle, Nallur circle, Kopay circle, Uduvil circle, Sandilipay circle, Sanganai circle and Tellippalai circle, Tellippalai circle was non-functional. The people in that area had left their houses and moved away. The civilians had moved away because the other districts in Valikamam were under threat by the army base in Palali. As a result, they had become ghost towns, with absolutely no human traffic.

When the Sri Lankan army captured many of the smaller islands in 1991, a large population had been displaced; they were now living in camps set up in the Valikamam areas. The Island Division of the political cadres took up projects among them. These people

Thamizhini in Vanni Training Camp

had suffered numerous abuses under the military, and there were many tearful stories among them.

Our main projects in Valikamam were: organizing monthly commemoration events for the War Heroes, meeting with the people from the villages, recruiting new members for the Movement, selling the Movement newspapers 'Liberation Tigers' and 'Freedom Birds' door to door, organizing funeral arrangements for the fallen fighters, and from time to time taking up essential work to meet the needs of the Movement. Because I was involved in all this work, I had the opportunity of getting to know different places and people with all kinds of different personalities. Truly, I came to understand that taking every opportunity to get to know the people and learn about their joy and grief would help us mature further. During that time, the Tiger police set up divisional stations and went into operation. Hitherto, the people's complaints had been dealt with by the political cadres. We were informed afterward that any complaints brought to our base needed to be directed to the police station.

At the district level, some work was separately and specifically assigned to female cadres. Beyond that, I had suggested female cadres also be assigned responsibilities in the general projects being undertaken among the people and faced some opposition and conflict with many male officials.

There was a 'Political Science School' set up in Irupalai for the political cadres. All the members gathered there for the classes they conducted. The political science courses were conducted by senior members and other important officials. They also conducted speech contests, debates and general knowledge tests there. These were educational opportunities for the members of the Movement, as well as arenas where they could unearth their talents.

Cadres were selected to form a new Education Division. A total of 10 people, both men and women, were selected. The head of the Political Front, Thamilselvan, selected each Education Division cadre with the expectation that they would conduct themselves in the manner of an officer. Some who had experience leading troops on the battlefield, and others who had done political work among the people were selected. I was selected for that division as well. The cadres were ready to pack up and their clothes and leave for whatever work they were given in the Movement. I did the same as well.

Time rushed by like a forest river that cannot stop to contemplate. I served within the LTTE Movement, which had been built as a rigid institution, at a time when it was at the very height of its surge. It was beyond even our dreams to distinguish between right and wrong in the actions and decisions of the Movement, or to subject them to any kind of intense scrutiny. Beyond this, our fighters were giving up their lives without any questions on the frontlines. Nothing could stand in the face of those sacrifices. I had no other aspirations than to fulfil my duty as a faithful fighter until I died 'The Hero's death'. The river of time swiftly flowed, closing over every hill and hollow.

4

The Tamil People and the Armed Conflict

We all stood around the model of a massive military base and an enlarged map. The special brigadier of the women's unit stood in front of us and pointed to the model.

'Anyone know where this place is? Let me see if you can tell us,' she said as she faced the fighters standing there. The model depicted an army base near the sea, situated in an arid zone, like those found close to the shore.

'Elephant Pass', 'Mullaitivu', 'No, no, it has to be Elephant Pass.' The cadres came up with different opinions and guesses. The brigadier, who had been watching us all silently, motioned for us to be quiet.

'Okay everyone, look closely. This is the map of the Poonakari military base. We have been training all these days with the aim to attack and destroy the Poonakari military base. The base is surrounded by land and sea. So, the Movement has come up with a strategy to launch simultaneous attacks on the base, by land and sea.'

Around the end of 1993, our unit had been receiving our training in a replica of an army base, in the lagoon adjoining Vallaiveli, in the Acchuveli area. It was only now that we understood which army base on the model depicted. The strike on Poonakari military base was the first major attack I was involved in.

I was appointed in charge of a unit of 15 fighters. Our units were being trained rigorously day and night without a break. Major Sumangala from Trincomalee led our unit, which consisted of 45 fighters in total.

The Liberation Tigers had undertaken preparations for this attack for more than a year. Strike units consisting of more than 5000 fighters, including from the districts of Jaffna and Vanni, had been trained and engaged during this time. About 1000 women fighters alone were prepared for this battle. Women fighters had been involved in the reconnaissance operations on the Poonakari military base from the beginning. The female cadres of the Sea Tigers were involved to a large extent in the sea attack operations as well. In addition to the months of arduous special training, top-secret defence manoeuvres were undertaken as well.

By destroying the Poonakari military base, the Tigers' intention was to weaken the military base in Elephant Pass, which was the entrance to Jaffna, keep the Kilali lagoon route under the Tigers' control, and to frustrate the Sri Lankan Army's plan to capture Jaffna in its entirety.

Malathi Brigade special Brigadier Vithusha with fighters, including Thamizhini

It was the first time in the Tigers' strike history that they would be conducting an amphibious attack on a combined military-naval base. So, the Movement referred to the strike as 'Operation Frog'.

Pottu Amman, who was the Tigers' Head of Intelligence, supervised the organization of the operation. I had met Pottu Amman in person many times, but the training for the Poonakari attack gave me the first opportunity to learn attack strategy directly from him.

The units stationed in Jaffna were moved to Vanni through the Kilali lagoon. We were crammed into trucks night after night and taken to a camp situated near Ambakamam forest. The final preparations for the strike took place there, over two days. All the fighters were issued sack caps, extra rounds of ammunition, hand grenades, secret codes for radio communication, extra batteries for our walkie-talkies and dry rations.

Many of the fighters wrote their last messages for their families. Many of my closest friends participated in this strike. Each had their own dreams, hopes, doubts, a sense that survival was not guaranteed, and a frustration that could not be expressed. It was not hard to understand the many emotions brimming in the eyes of fighters in the final moments before going into a preordained battle. None of us could either speak of a future battle, or even imagine one.

The paddy fields of Poonakari and the relentless November rains had turned the battle that had begun on 11 November 1993 into a gruelling fight. Within three days of the start of the battle, more than 500 fighters died Heroes' deaths. However, for the first time in the history of the Movement a Sri Lankan army tank had been seized by the Tigers.

My unit was commanded to level the bunkers and clear the concertina barbed wire in between, in order to transport the tank from Poonakari into the Tigers' territory. Many other fighters worked with me at a furious pace to flatten the path, and within minutes of finishing, the battle tank rumbled noisily past us. A number of male cadres climbed onto the tank and waved the Tiger flag and cheered loudly as they went. Our hearts too rejoiced in the glow of victory at the sight.

After finally defeating Napoleon, the Duke of Wellington surveyed the battlefield at Waterloo, and said: 'Next to a battle lost, the saddest thing is a battle won.' For the first time in my life I experienced this sorrow. Many of the friends who had been very close to me, as dear to me as my life from the time I had stepped out of the house and joined the Movement, had been lost before my very eyes. Of them, Saampavi was my dearest friend. One of the brightest students in Jaffna's Chundikuli girls' school, she had walked past the tear-stained faces of many of her teachers to join the movement in 1991. She received combat training in the 23rd troop in Major Sothiya Base. Her experiences at the training base, would evoke tears, in spite of her superior leadership qualities, and the clarity of thought she demonstrated from an early age.

A few instructors in that training base provided prime examples of the kind of violations that happen when small-minded or perverse people were given authority and weapons in their hands. Those who had come for weapons training after serving as political aides were subjected to the most rigorous drilling, regardless of their age. Incidents of cadres receiving kicks and blows to the point of drawing blood, and being subjected to verbal abuse and personal vendettas, became the norm in that women's training base, and set a terrible example for the female combatants.

Saampavi and I were advancing, crouched in the paddy fields. They were flooded because of the continuous rainfall. The bullets of an army sniper situated on high ground in the distance did not miss their mark and drank up the lives of many fighters in that paddy field. We were crouched in those muddy fields without any way of sticking our heads up to get a look. Saampavi was crawling along beside me when suddenly I heard a weird sound: 'huc'. I turned around to look. Her face was buried in the mud. When I raised her head, I saw blood trickle from the corners of her mouth. A single bullet had struck her in the chest and lodged near her heart. I felt the last lingering traces of her life's warmth in my hands, as her body grew cold.

Saampavi had not anticipated in the least that she could be killed in this battle. 'When this battle is done, I want to go look around

Vanni with you. We must write down our experiences in a book.' She had many such dreams and desires.

Thamarai was another friend who lost her life, shot in the head in that same paddy field. Her eyes captured everyone, though she was quiet and barely spoke. It had often struck me that an unrelenting sadness dwelt in those eyes. The night before the battle began, our troop had been stationed in the fourth sector of Poonakari and we were spending the last night there. The focus search beams from the military base kept circling the area, turning the district into daytime. PAR lamps were also glaring down on us from a height. One of the members of our troop was singing in a soft voice. As she sang the words 'In that moment, when your soul departs, who did you think of', my mother's face moved through my mind.

I turned to Thamarai, who was seated next to me, and asked: 'Whom would you think of, Thamarai?' Her downcast eyes glittered briefly. A slight smile trembled on her chapped lips. 'I will only think of the one I loved.' I can't remember the name she said. But it was the only time she revealed the wound of the love she had buried deep within herself. Her beloved, also a fighter, had already died in some battle.

In this way, prolonged with innumerable tearful stories, the Poonakari battle gained a massive victory for the LTTE. The Tigers celebrated great victories in capturing the high-speed naval gunboats and heavy weaponry.

The Sri Lankan army had suffered heavy casualties as well. The image of another unforgettable sight I witnessed there, is deeply imprinted on my memory. The lifeless bodies of the soldiers and cadres lay stiffening, soaked in rainwater. The red of their blood dissolved slowly in the rain and ebbed away. They, who had stood face to face at war with each other just a few moments ago, full of an unquenchable hatred, now evoked a vision of children sleeping sprawled on a mother's lap. At that time, I didn't have the wisdom to understand that the battlefield could also be a place where all differences, oppressions and enmities would lose all meaning.

More than a thousand fighters, including Political Aide Thamilselvan and Brigadier Sornam, had been injured in the battle. Three days later, our troops had withdrawn from Poonakari. All the fighters who had participated in this battle had been given a week's leave. I had gone home on leave for the first time since I had joined the movement. Though there had been many changes in my family in the three years or so that I had been away, they embraced me and showered me with love. When it was time for me to return to the base after leave, they turned away from me, silently and tearfully. Though it hurt to leave my family again, the thought of my friends who had given their lives pulled me back to the path of the struggle.

The 'Lingam' base, which had been set up as a women's vanguard base by Mahattaya, had been changed to the Political Secretariat of Political Aide Thamilselvan. The political school had been set up in another section of the compound. There were separate houses for the male and female cadres as well. As Jaffna College fell within its perimeter, I had the opportunity to attend many valuable public education events that were held at the Kailasapathy auditorium there. In the middle of 1993, I was able to attend a journalism course that was held there and learned some valuable lessons in media studies.

The cadres of the Education Division were taught many invaluable lessons by prominent members of the movement and by professors appointed by the movement. Though we were taught about the Movement's history, the history of freedom struggles around the world, social sciences and general knowledge by instructors from the fields, nothing remained consistent. The Education Division cadres were often used as special troops in the Movement's propaganda campaigns. So, our classes were often disrupted.

In 1994, the Tiger movement had undertaken large-scale propaganda activities in Yazh district. The Poonakari period had raised the people's expectations of the Tigers. At the same time, many skilled senior fighters were arrested on charges of having conspired with Mahattaya. There were many changes in responsibilities in the Political wing as well.

At this time, a gathering of the senior and intermediate officers, and brigadiers of the Movement was organized by the Intelligence Division at the Irupalai Political Academy. We cadres from the Political Wing participated in that gathering as well. A few cadres were handcuffed and lined up on the stage. I knew one person in that lineup; the others were strangers to me. I only knew the fighter called Suseelan anna, from my early schooldays, when he used to come around on a bicycle, wearing a sarong. He was light-skinned and quite tall. I had heard him spoken of among the fighters as the one who had skilfully driven the captured battle tank across, though he had no previous experience in driving one. He was known to everyone as a highly skilled combatant. I couldn't believe he could have committed a major infraction. An officer from the Intelligence Division read out the charges against them.

It was said that the deputy head of the movement, Mahattaya, had become an agent of the Indian spy organization RAW, acted against the Leader, and that these fighters had abetted in those activities. It was also said that 'Kiruban', who had escaped from prison in India, had been used by RAW for their own purposes; that though he claimed to have escaped from the prison, he had in fact been sent to assassinate the Leader; and that he had returned to the movement with the intention of gaining our trust and carrying out his plan. They also said that these fighters had attempted to poison the Leader and had placed a bomb in his car at Mahattaya's instigation.

They also informed us that there had been a plan to assassinate the Leader when he had planned a visit to inaugurate the memorial established at Kodikamam, to honour the Heroes who died in the battle of Elephant Pass; that there had been weapons stashed for the purpose, and the plot had failed when the Leader did not appear at the event as planned.

I remembered there had been some hubbub of 'anna is coming' to Kodikamam, and for some reason Pottu Amman showed up for the opening at the last minute.

At that time, it was only Mahattaya who had the authority to carry his pistol in the Leader's presence. They told us that the full RAW conspiracy was to have Mahattaya shoot the Leader with his own handgun; Kiruban would seemingly react in anger, immediately shooting and killing him. The fighters would be convinced that Kiruban had shot the traitor Mahattaya out of his loyalty to the Leader, and thereby accept him as the new leader. It was announced in that gathering that the plot to turn the Liberation Tigers into a puppet of RAW had been quashed.

Discipline was tight for the fighters in the Movement. Infractions like fraud and sexual crimes were punished most severely, with a death sentence. But Mahattaya, who had been the Deputy Leader of the movement had not only refrained from punishing the cadres in his charge who indulged in these crimes, but had then turned them into his accomplices, by threatening to inform the Leader of their actions. The agreement was that he would protect them if they cooperated with him, we were told.

The accused who were handcuffed in that gathering rose one by one and admitted to their crimes. The fighters who were gathered there stood as still as statues. As far as I was concerned, I had thought of the Movement as a family brought together by a shared ideal. When I learned of these things, I was so frightened and confused, I could hardly breathe. I could sense that many of the fighters were as stunned as I was. Some, who could not contain their feelings, began crying quietly; some stood up, faced the accused and began to berate them furiously. This turned out to be one of the most traumatic events for the fighters of that time. The 'Mahattaya affair' sent shockwaves through the civilian population as well. He had enjoyed a wonderful reputation among them and had been known to have worked extremely hard to keep the Movement growing in some of its hardest times.

The people raised many questions about the Mahattaya affair at the Current Politics conferences organized by the Political Wing. 'Where is Mahattaya?' the people would demand angrily. We were told to inform the people that he was under suspicion for planning the assassination of the Leader, and had been arrested, and that an inquiry was taking place.

During the gatherings I participated in during 1992–93, the people would launch a barrage of questions at the Tigers: 'Why were the Muslims expelled from the north?', 'Why were the fighters in other groups wiped out by the LTTE?' and other similar questions took us aback many times, as we were fairly new to the Movement. To be honest, we barely knew the answers to those questions ourselves.

The people observed the political events continuously and bore the whole burden of the struggle as well. We had to keep faith with them, because we were fighting on their behalf. It's true that many rebels intended that our operations would be satisfactory to the people. But at times when our activities created difficulties for the people, we saw them as sacrifices, unavoidable in a time of war.

The fighters of the LTTE were never given a proper explanation for why the other Movements were wiped out by the Tigers. Instead, the idea gained credence within the Movement that the other Movements were stopped because of their wrongdoings. When new recruits were filling out their registration forms, they had to state whether they had any siblings or relatives in any of the other groups. In the period after 2000, a notable few of the dead from other Movements, were included in the list of War Heroes. From what I knew, the female combatant Usha, who had belonged to the EPRLF and lost her life in a battle with the army at Kokavil, was added to the list of War Heroes. I don't know any details about her beyond that, or when that incident had taken place.

During the 2002 Peace Process, the LTTE conducted peace talks and reached agreements with Muslim politicians, after which there were some Muslims who returned to their own homes. I too had the opportunity of meeting with Muslims in Nachchikuda, which was in the Tiger-controlled area of Mulanga, in the Mannar district; in Neeravi Piddi; in Mulliyavalai in the Mullaitivu district; and the five-junction area of Jaffna. When I met these people, whose livelihood depended on sea and land, and who lived such ordinary lives, I felt a tremendous sense of guilt within my heart. I couldn't accept, in my heart, that there was any justice in our Movement subjecting these innocent people's livelihood to such oppression, when we claimed to be fighting oppression ourselves.

Towards the end of 1994, the Movement's forces were gathered and began training for a massive strike. Troops began training in various locations in Jaffna district. Cadres from the political wing were sent for training as well. Training for the female fighters took place in Ariyaalai in Maniyanthottam. It was explained to us that we'd have to go out to sea, up to a certain distance by boat, then walk through neck deep water, and then launch our attack. They said that the attack would be full of challenges, as we'd have to carry the injured back through the water as well.

While the preparations for the final stages of the attack on the military base in Mandaitivu were being carried out, the vehicles arrived to transport our troops. It was around seven at night. The troops were prepared to climb into the vehicles. After some sudden message came in, we were told the operation was cancelled, and we were sent back to our quarters. We were not informed why that operation had been abandoned. We did learn that some espionage data had been leaked to the military. Our troop was sent back to political work.

Following this, in the beginning of 1995, a massive strike was planned to simultaneously hit the five military bases Kokkilai, Kokku Thoduvai, Karunaattukkeni, Dollar Farm and Kent Farm in the Manal Aru area. The Leopard Brigade, which was carefully trained under the close and careful supervision of the Leader himself, was largely involved in this attack. Even other members of the Movement could not see them. They would have no leave for the first five years of service. They were put through year-long sessions of combat training and were taught military stratagem. It was the custom of the women of that brigade to keep their hair cut short. They were also taught the arts of self-defence, like karate, wrestling, and boxing. My younger sister was a member of the Leopard Brigade as well.

The attack did not go through as the Movement had hoped. On the contrary, it brought massive losses to us. The Leopard Brigade, the Leader's dream brigade, had met with destruction. More than 200 male and female combatants lost their lives, and their shattered bodies were delivered by the Sri Lankan government to the Tigers, through the ICRC.

At that time, I was serving in the Vadamaradchi area. We received news that the massive strike launched by the Leopard Brigade had met with defeat, and that many female combatants had lost their lives. I kept quiet and submerged myself in my work, even though I was frantic, not knowing if my sister had participated in this offensive or not.

The Vadamaradchi sector was also sent a list of names of the deceased, so we could inform their families. Thinking about the work could make you feel dizzy and collapse. How could we possibly take the news of their death to their parents, who had been suffering at not having seen their children for five years? At that time, I thought of my mother. Not having seen my sister in over four years, what pain, tears and despair would she undergo if she heard news like this?

What could we do? When we took on the burden of this order, searched for their addresses, and went to their homes trembling with fear, a deluge burst upon us. Some parents embraced us as they wept; some others beat us and swore and threatened us in their anguish. There was nothing we could do but join them in their weeping.

More than 50 bodies were sent to Vadamaradchi for their last rites. They were taken directly to the funeral grounds. They were neither identifiable, nor were they in any decent shape to be delivered to their parents. The wailing of mothers who went from one coffin to another, not knowing which of the row of coffins set out in the burial grounds held their child, still echoes in my ears.

Early that same year, the Sri Lankan Army undertook Operation Leap Forward through Chandalippay, in the eastern area of Valikamam. The Tigers launched a counterattack to stop it in its tracks. During the air force attack at that time, the Navali church (St. Peter's) was struck. Many civilians taking refuge there were killed. The sight of little children twitching in pools of blood should never be seen again, not only in our nation, but in any corner of the world.

At that time, many young men and women joined the Tigers' Movement in large numbers. The rebel training base grounds were filled to overflowing. Many new female troops began training for marine and land attacks.

In the middle of October 1995, the Sri Lankan army launched Operation Riviresa (sun ray), with the intention of capturing the entirety of Jaffna. Using the Palali Joint Military Headquarters as their rearguard, the Sri Lankan troops began advancing. At first the Tigers' Jaffna district attack troops launched counterstrikes. Every day, the army attacks escalated. As the army began to advance in stages, the Tigers brought together their full force to fight. The rebel casualties mounted daily. Those of us who were engaged in projects with the civilian population, were organizing the Heroes' memorial events.

When the army captured Vadamaradchi and accelerated their plan to fully capture Valikamam, the Leader made an unexpected and abrupt decision. The civilians were hurriedly informed, through loudspeakers, that they had to evacuate Valikamam immediately. Whether they liked it or not, the people paid heed to the announcement, picked up what belongings they could carry, and began to make their way towards the Navatkuli bridge. It must be said that no matter how hard you try, it's impossible to express the great human calamity of half a million people leaving behind their homes, their properties, their gardens, their pets, everything behind in a few hours and crossing the Navatkuli bridge. Some other cadres and I stayed in Thenmaradchi, offering what help we could to those people.

The Movement explained that this decision was made with the intention of preventing civilian casualties in the skirmishes between the army and the Tigers. Yet, the suffering of those people, and the price they paid, cannot be discounted. Thenmaradchi district was now full of civilians. The schools, churches and houses were filled to overflowing, and the gardens, lanes and streets were also filled. The rain poured relentlessly.

The Tigers saw it as a political victory for themselves that the people accepted their order and evacuated Jaffna. They felt they had gained some international recognition, because the UN and other international groups would now have to communicate through the Tigers in order to offer any kind of aid to civilians. The Movement announced the event to the world as a sign that the Tamil people were completely behind the Tigers.

The Tigers believed that, though the Sri Lankan military had fully captured Jaffna district, to have captured an unpopulated area was a political failure; that it would be impossible for the army to maintain its hold over an area that was deserted but full of buildings, and that they would be forced to retreat.

At the time that Jaffna was lost, important images and documents were transported to Vanni through Kilali and Kadaleri. The people were asked to move to Vanni as well. A large population moved towards Vanni. Some stayed on in Thenmaradchi. At that time many youths, young women and university students joined the Movement.

The Sri Lankan army employed covert manoeuvres to capture the Kanakampuliyadi junction in Thenmaradchi. Following this, the army captured the entirety of Thenmaradchi. A huge number of civilians ignored the air force's aerial bombardment and moved to Vanni, through the Kilali lagoon. People who had no knowledge of Vanni at all up until then, journeyed to Vanni, with who knows what hope. Another segment of the population stayed in Thenmaradchi, determined to return to their own homes one day.

Though the Tigers had no desire for these people to return under military occupation, their hands were tied, and they were helpless to prevent them from doing so. At the same time, it was believed that if the Tigers wanted to continue their attacks to disrupt the military forces that were now permanently stationed in Jaffna district, having people living in the military-controlled areas would prove to be useful.

The last day I spent walking with Vithusha akka through the abandoned Chavakachcheri junction was unforgettable. The Kilali beach, that had been the travel route for the mass exodus to Vanni, was as bare as the streets after a temple festival. I climbed and sat in one of the remaining boats and gazed at the shores of Jaffna's Thenmaradchi, until they disappeared from my sight. I couldn't bear to think of the beautiful town, and its people's lives so cruelly shattered and laid to waste by war. People who had lived as close together as banana trees, which sprout shoots in their own shade, had been plucked out root and soil by this war.

5

The Female Fighter and an Unchanged Society

'For 20 years I was in the Movement. I had been injured in so many battles, I only knew how to lead assault brigades and to carry and fire a gun. What am I going to do when I go home now?'

'When I wore the camouflage uniform and walked into town with a gun, everyone looked at me with some awe in their eyes. People thought of me and treated me as their own child because I was fighting for them. Now I go into the town. No gun, no uniform, no decent clothes to wear on a regular basis. Because I have never earned anything for myself. Now people turn their faces away when they see me, or they sneer at me. I hear voices behind my back, "These ones could have bitten the cyanide (capsule) rather than come back alive." Like a dud coin, I have no value.'

'This one was in the Movement then. Now she's working with the army, and the ones who go that way don't have a good reputation.'

I ask myself why I begin this chapter this way. Isn't this the reality of today? We female fighters dreamed of bending the sky to a bow once. Now, all our dreams are dissolved, and we lie fallen at the threshold of reality.

The participation and dedication of female fighters in the armed struggle went contrary to the norms of our society. Just as the Liberation Tigers' Movement had built itself up as its own unique social order, so the founding of the female fighters had been completely and uniquely removed from society. Our society watched the female fighters from an amused distance, praising us with a mixture of disbelief and awe.

It had become necessary for the people to accept the path of the separatist struggle which had been put forward by the Tamil political leaders, no matter what their criticisms might have been. The impact of the state of exception created by the armed struggle compelled society to tolerate and come to accept women who bore arms as well. For this reason, the ridicule that originally arose when women first went into battle diminished over time and eventually dissipated.

Another factor, when it came to Tamil society, was that though Tamil women were raised within an oppressive belief structure, their unique strength of character continued to manifest itself within the constraints of the family. Even if they did not socialize much, or were largely uneducated, their authority and capacity for managing finances in the family had strengthened them to be load-bearers of their families in times of emergency.

In those times, when the fundamental rights of the average person were denied, their familiarity with oppression became the very reason women were able to endure and develop the inner strength to survive the impact of the crises that faced them. It was as an extension of this, that from the beginning of the struggle they stepped out with courage into the street, to enter into armed combat for the liberation of their people. Many women who had an in-depth knowledge of politics and society surpassed the boundaries they left behind to enter the political realm in the Movement. The bitter truth of it is, we women taught ourselves that we could accomplish more, in terms of strengthening our position in society, through taking up arms in battle rather than through bringing about changes in the education and thinking of women.

During my school years, the Tigers had grown into the majoritarian liberation Movement. The female brigades were accomplishing brave feats and sacrificing their lives on the battlefronts. Though I primarily joined the Movement because we were in a state of war, as a woman I also thought of it as an opportunity to rebel and shatter the stereotypes of womanhood held by my family and the community around me. When I joined the Movement at that school-going age, I felt some thrill and excitement, but I think at that time I had no understanding of politics or society.

In the period 1989–92, female fighters joined the Movement in the thousands. At this time, rudimentary weapons training camps would be run side by side, with 300 female instructors each. With the Sugi training base in Polikandy, Jaffna, Jeevan and Castro training bases in Manal Aru forest, Kilali, Sothiya and Thilaka in Thenmaradchi, and beyond this, in 1992, the Leopard Brigade, the female Sea Tigers Unit, and other brigades, the Tigers' Movement was growing at a rate previously unseen anywhere in the world.

It is questionable to what extent women were able to change their fundamental thinking, though they were certainly able to prove their physical strength when they received combat training. It can't be said that all the women who left behind the familial institution and entered the institution of the Movement were revolutionary and underwent some change in thought. Just as we were raised to be docile in the family, so we were raised to be obedient female fighters of the Movement, with rigorous military training.

The state of mind of the Tamil woman who wears the camouflage uniform and carries a weapon in her hand is entirely different. The mental transformation she undergoes when she understands that she can protect herself; that she can redeem herself from the social constraints she has known from her birth, and comes to value herself; that when duties and responsibilities are given to her she may have the opportunity to make independent decisions; and the sense of dedication she feels above all things, mark an important phase in her life. We were spurred on in the most rigorous combat training by the thought that we women of Eelam would one day write stories of bravery, like the women who joined the battle in the Chinese Red Army, in Palestine and in Telangana. However, it was unfortunate that the Movement lacked the practices to direct these ideals so they could take shape as a transformative change in our nature rather than remain temporary experiences.

We did not have any long-range principles or plans for the liberation of women. We dreamed a dream that because we stepped outside the house and picked up arms that we could somehow change society. But the fact of the matter is, though we were able to achieve many victories on the battlefield as a result of women carrying arms and entering into combat, there was absolutely no change in the notions our society held regarding women. The heady rush for the liberation of women in Tamil society began with the image of the female fighter and ended with defeat in the war.

'It is the improvement of the educational and economic conditions of women, and the respect of a mutual humanity beyond male female gender differences, that will make the liberation of women a reality.' The Leader of the Movement often expressed this principle in various forms in his statements released on occasions like Women's Day.

The work of the Women's Political Wing was to enlighten the community about the rights of women, to improve the living conditions of women, to seek out affected women in the community and offer them rehabilitation, and to work for societal change in an expanded form. It was on this basis that project measures were set out for the Women's Political Wing. In reality, our activities became limited to recruiting new fighters for the Movement and to completing the specific tasks assigned to women. This was because the entire focus of the Movement, and all its resources, was directed at the aim of winning the war.

In 1999, the war in Vanni had reached peak intensity. The propaganda division of the political wing worked to recruit new fighters to the Movement. A senior male fighter was set in charge of it. Both male and female fighters worked together with him. Throughout the months, they had the responsibility of bringing in a certain number of youths and girls to join up as fighters. With this aim they conducted street theatre, conferences, warrior drumming events, and even met with people individually. I was given the huge responsibility of being the speaker for these events. I had said there that it was only through participating in the armed conflict that women could bring about real change in society. And yet,

I couldn't say that along with armed combat there was a parallel programme undertaken to bring about those changes in society. The responsibilities and activities of female fighters had begun to expand a great deal. The Women's Wing was established as a separate administrative division and many brigades and divisions were formed. They began operating in the expanded frontlines and the rearguard. New female colonels and commanders were appointed. However, as a result, the camaraderie and togetherness that had existed at the beginning began to diminish. The uniformity of the administrative work gave way to changes in the Women's Wing.

The first training base for female fighters of the LTTE began on 18 August 1985 in Dindigul, in the Sirumalai region of Tamil Nadu. There, Ponnammaan, the best instructor in the Movement provided six months of extremely rigorous training to the female cadres. In the second team that followed, in Kilali, Jaffna, female fighters provided the training themselves. The female colonels did not like male commanders sticking their noses in any level of the female fighters' administration. From the beginning, the Leader himself guided all matters relating to the female fighters personally. It is an undeniable fact that the female fighters showed the Leader the affection and familiarity in behaviour they usually reserved for their fathers at home.

Though male and female fighters could receive training together and undertake tasks together, the penalties for violating the stringent codes of moral conduct were extremely harsh. In this way the Movement was a fortress of safety for the female fighters. It's not as though there weren't any transgressions. The Movement undertook measures to eradicate those as well. In January of 1993, all the female fighters were brought together at the Sothiya base in Kilali where the execution of three female fighters was carried out in front of them. This execution was carried out in keeping with the Criminal Procedure Code of the Movement, because these women, who had been living in the Vadamaradchi base, had engaged in sexual relations with men outside the Movement. The men associated with the crime were also condemned and executed in a public place.

The female colonels wished to create strong bonds between the female fighters, and with this intention wanted to unite the female regiments to create a Women's Council. When this was put forward to the Leader, he welcomed the idea and expressed his wish to participate in the organization and to share his thoughts as well. Brigadier Vithusha was put in charge of the organization, second to her was Brigadier Thurka; I was appointed as secretary, and senior member Janani was appointed treasurer. The Leader had given Brigadier Vithusha 50,000 rupees for the operating costs of the Women's Council.

A manifesto on the practices of the female cadres was created for this organization. We carried out a general assessment of the needs and concerns of the female fighters and put forward some solutions. As the Council's reports were sent directly to the Leader, all the other colonels in the female cadres' administration took great care in their participation. As women were engaged in important tasks at the frontlines as well as elsewhere, it became necessary to give room to the thoughts of female commanders and colonels as well.

Many problems also arose around the marriages of female cadres, and their continued activities after marriage. Romantic and marital relations between male and female fighters were permitted within the Movement. The Leader appointed political advisor Anton Balasingham as the head of the marriage administration in the Liberation Tigers in 1991. He quit the position the very next year, saying that he could not fulfil the responsibility. Referring to his reasons much later, he said: 'There are many older women in the Movement, women who have been injured in battle, fighters who have lost limbs. It is the male cadres in the Movement who should come forward to marry them. Some of our boys don't think of marrying the women cadres who fought beside them in the battlefield but go roaming in search of girls who are pretty, have good jobs, or have relatives abroad. I told the Leader that I am not needed to carry out these kinds of marriages, and I left.'

After this time, priority was given to marriages between two cadres who had served in the Movement. The higher-ups in command chose to marry women fighters from within the Movement.

Among other ranks as well, love and marriage took place normally. When members fell in love, they had to inform the Chief Secretariat through their respective commanders. To engage in sexual relations before marriage was a crime that carried a severe penalty. The marriageable age for men was 29, and for women 23. It was expected that at least one of the two had to have served for at least five years in the Movement.

When a few fighters got married, there were covert caste-based enquiries as well. But many fighters surpassed these boundaries to marry and begin loving lives together. In my family, my maternal grandmother was in the habit of observing caste. I had noticed her only giving a bottle with drinking water to a man who worked at our place. One time, when he asked for some water, I gave him water in a tumbler we used, right in front of my grandmother. Ammamma was extremely angry, but she threw the tumbler outside without even a word to me. It was then that I came to realize how big a problem caste was within our society.

When I went to do political work among the people in Jaffna, as a member of the Movement, it burned me to see the oppressiveness of even highly educated people trapped in the gutter of caste practice. Through the writings of K. Daniel, I had come to understand the ways in which caste oppression was embedded in our society. I would talk to my friends among the female cadres about the need to work with the people to raise consciousness around caste when we liberated our own nation. Many fighters completely despised caste practice. They understood the urgency to rebel against it. However, though they may have undergone combat training, some underwent no changes deep in their hearts as far as their beliefs went regarding caste, religion, unnecessary traditions, and superstitions.

In this situation, difficult predicaments often arose when many older male fighters requested permission to marry very young female fighters. However, the final deciding authority rested with the female commanders in this matter. It was also common that conflicts arose when male colonels tried to apply pressure on behalf of their cadres. This created a lot of stress for the female commanders as well. I was given the task of creating a focus group to form a nursery to care for the children born to the married cadres when they returned to service. The first nursery 'Thalir Children's Nursery' was set up in Puthukkudiyiruppu.

At the same time, many female fighters remained unmarried, though they were either roughly past marrying age, badly injured or had lost limbs. They were so completely immersed in their unending work for the Movement that they did not stop to think that they were getting older, or that they should find life partners for themselves. The Movement had given them safety, met their basic needs and given them the prestige of being a fighter. Some of the female fighters I knew wanted to continue in the Movement and had no intention of getting married. In this way the Movement had given them some measure of independence as well.

Though a vast number of female combatants served on the battlefield, division command was usually reserved for male colonels. Only female colonels with a long history of battle experience were appointed by the Leader to command divisions of male or female fighters. Frontline divisions had been given to the charge of Brigadier Vithusha and Brigadier Thurka. So, the female fighters of the Tigers saw some advancement within the military framework.

In May of 1992, women in leading positions in the Liberation Tigers organized a women's conference at the Windsor Theatre in Jaffna and decided on 10 important proposals. The most important of these was the 'dowry ban'. As far as Tamil society was concerned, this practice was a problem that affected not only women, but also the entire society. After doing some social research on the matter, the 'law banning the practice of dowry (marriage gift)' was passed by the Tamil Eelam Judicial Division. However, as far as practice went, the law remained dormant and gathered dust in the Tigers' Judicial Division.

Female fighters were active as judges and lawyers, were engaged in legal work, and participated in media in the documentary and film division, newspapers, and broadcasting. Many female fighters were innovative writers and thought beyond armed combat about wider concepts in the social and political fields. However, their creations and expressions could not exceed the bounds of the Movement's creeds and could only serve to buttress the tenets of the struggle.

The Liberation Tigers Movement outgrew its origins as a guerilla movement and turned into a traditional army, and in its final days became its own society. In the end, the fighters, their families, children, the elders in their care (the parents of the great Heroes), the children in Sencholai, Kantharuban, Arivu Cholai and in rehabilitation, orphaned women, elders, men and women with mental health issues, were all abandoned. The Movement had taken no measures to protect them.

The condition of the female fighters in the last days of Mullivaikkal was most pitiful. There was no way out for many of them except to commit suicide wherever they found themselves. The female cadres of the Sea Tigers had been stationed in the Mullivaikkal region with vehicles loaded with explosives and wearing explosive belts awaiting orders from Colonel Soosai of the Sea Tigers. Many injured female cadres took cyanide and died within the bunkers. Many female fighters stood around in their stations, in utter confusion as to what was going to happen to them. There was no general statement given to the fighters. I had not heard of any female fighters being included in the last-ditch effort to get the Leader and some of the Colonels to escape through Nanthikadal.

How terrible is the present condition of women in our society who took up arms to fight for the homeland? Because they escaped with their lives one day, they must go through the anguish of a living death every day. The economic hardships, the lingering trauma of their battle experiences, the criticisms of society, the difficulties finding a suitable life-partner—the troubles women face for the crime of having gone to battle exceed all bounds. It is the natural endurance of Tamil women, an attitude of fighting in the face of adversity, and the courage they had learned on the battlefield that strengthens them today to take the battle of their lives forward. And yet, the next generation is formed bearing their psychological damage.

A woman I know had been injured in the stomach during the war; her parents had arranged an overseas groom for her. We learned that as she had been injured in the stomach, the groom had informed them that he would make his decision about the match only after he had examined her medical X-rays. If she was unable to bear a child, she would also be unable to become a life partner. A society that ordinarily does not accept any flaws or faults in a woman as a life-partner, is a tremendous obstacle to the prospects of family life for the female fighter, who has been seriously injured in the frontlines of a war. It was not wrong that they went into battle; it was wrong that they returned alive. This is the battlefield of society that the former female combatant faces. Time passes all those by who have found victory here, and those who have stumbled, and keeps moving on.

6

Memories of the Eastern Soil

When the tsunami struck the shores of Sri Lanka at the end of 2004, many coastal villages in the North and East were completely destroyed. When this natural disaster struck, I was stationed in the Mannar town area, working on political projects in our base. The head tribunal sent us a message that many people who had been injured in the tsunami were in desperate need of blood transfusions, and that we must make immediate arrangements for this, and send the blood to Mullaitivu.

Though I had seen the terrible destruction of war face to face, I could not have imagined nature rise up and swallow people in such a display of force. When the civilians showed up like an army at the Mannar general hospital after hearing the announcements on our loudspeakers calling on them to give blood to save the lives of our families, I felt the truth that human compassion for all humanity had not yet diminished. The coastal people also informed us that the waves of the Talaimannar sea were growing larger than normal. When we went to Talaimannar to investigate, we found women and children of Sinhala and Muslim fishing families, who lived in fishing huts in that area, shaken by the sight of the massive waves. We cleared them from the shores, brought them further inland and decided to house them in the school building there. We thought we could assess the conditions the next day and decide what to do with them.

I received a message asking me to come to Kilinochchi right away, and I rushed over. None of the cadres from the Political Wing were staying in their bases. They were all involved in emergency rescue measures for the affected people on the shores from the east of Vadamaradchi to Mullaitivu. The head of the Political Wing, Thamilselvan, had taken me with him to an emergency meeting to plan out these operations. Rescue operations to help the injured and to retrieve the bodies of the dead were underway at the same time. School buildings had been set up to accommodate the rescued survivors. They were putting together cooked food for the survivors, milk powder for the children, and other immediate necessities. The Tigers' troops were working closely with the people, at a furious pace.

The gathering I was supposed to participate in had been organized at Iyakachchi junction. As we were in the middle of a ceasefire at the time, members of the NGOs who were active in Vanni at the time, members of the district councils, officers of the Movement's Political Wing, and members of various religious orders were gathered under a tree beside the A9 highway. Thamilselvan asked them what urgent work they could undertake on behalf of their respective groups. While we were working to provide relief supplies to the civilians immediately, some NGOs expressed that they had to follow their usual channels and send plans to the head offices in Colombo for approval before they could act. Their argument angered the head of the Political Wing.

He said that it was best if those willing to undertake the urgent and vital measures needed in the face of this natural disaster could stay behind, and those who thought they could only act if they followed standard procedure could quit the area. That put several NGOs in a bind. Many organizations began to describe the immediate aid they could offer. It was decided that the NGOs active there would collaborate in carrying out the emergency measures set out by the People's Rehabilitation group.

In order to meet the basic needs of the women and children in the emergency shelters, female civilian helpers worked beside female cadres. A similar organizing meeting was held in the Mulliyavalai area for the people in the Mullaitivu district. As I had not personally been assigned any other tasks until the meetings were finished and we returned to Kilinochchi, I decided to go to the emergency shelters and work beside the other cadres.

When we reached the Peace Office in Kilinochchi, we learned that there had not been proper contact with the government officials in Batticaloa and Amparai. As we needed someone to leave for those places directly, Thamilselvan gave me the responsibility.

'Thamizhini! You must leave for Amparai immediately. On top of being hit by the waves, it has been raining non-stop, and there has been flooding as well. Twenty-five lorries have arrived with relief supplies from Jaffna, and you must take them with you. If you wait for an army escort you won't be able to head out in the morning. You'll be delayed...You'd have to go in secret, without them knowing. What do you say? Can you do it?'

My heart did not hesitate for a moment. 'Yes, I can. I'll go.'

I had some experience of going to the eastern province a few times for political work after the ceasefire. The first two times I went there, I had met with Karuna Amman, who was a Brigadier in the LTTE at the time. He also helped us a lot with the women's conference we had organized then. When the Movement was split, fighters in the Tigers' assault brigades had engaged in a war of brother against brother, with the aim of recouping cadres from the eastern province. After that, I was sent with a few other female cadres as part of a special propaganda team of political cadres to meet with the people of the eastern province. I have the most unforgettable memories of going door to door and speaking to people about their experiences in many areas, including Palukamam, Kaluvankeni, Kokkadicholai, Thandiyadi, Makiladithivu, Vakarai and Kathiraveli. Nothing in the world could compare with the affection they showed us, for no matter what pain or hardships they carried in their hearts, they greeted visitors at the door with: 'Come in, daughter, sit down. Eat, daughter. You look so tired, have at least a cup of water before you go, children.' Just as the beauty of nature embraced their soil, the people's hearts were full of humility and love.

When we had left the Vakarai area after finishing our propaganda work and turned towards Karadiyanaru, four cadres who were very familiar with the area went ahead of us on two motorbikes. A few minutes after they set off, they were hit by an unexpected Claymore attack and a male cadre lost his life, while a female cadre was seriously injured. The two survivors escaped through the forest and eventually reached us. In those conditions, for a fighter to go over from Vanni to serve in the eastern province was a challenge that carried the risk of death. It must not be forgotten that behind the military victories the Tigers attained in Vanni, were acts of fierce courage and sacrifice carried out by the fighters from the eastern province. The affection and care we received when we met with the people in the eastern province were also unstinted.

It's hard to look back on the sorrowful stories those people told us of the hardships they had undergone during the 'war between brothers' that was undertaken with the eastern fighters. When it got to the point that we had to put an end to the lives of those who had fought beside us for years, with our own hands, because of weak commanding officers trapped in an engine of lies; when it was thought beneath us to spare even the ordinary low ranking fighters who were caught up in circumstances beyond their control, because a stab in the back could never be forgiven; when the Movement slaughtered those fighters without a shred of mercy, that was when we all fell into that invisible engine of lies. I was put in a situation where I had to comfort the numerous parents who wept and complained that even the bodies of their children, who were slain in this terrible vendetta, had not been returned to them.

'Didn't our children go to fight for the nation? The Movement killed the children who went out there trusting in them,' they wept. How could I make those innocent parents understand the political rationale the Movement had given us? Those were times of great psychological turmoil. They were emotionally hard for me. To come to terms with the idea that a freedom struggle must go forward through these stages was like swallowing fire, not just for me, but for many of the fighters.

Female combatants had been stationed on the shores at Verukalaru. Malathi Brigade had been sent into the attack as well. Those days were a stain on the lives of the women who took up arms. We covered our mouths, speechless when the civilians told us how the eastern female cadres had been wandering around looking for protection, lost and in distress, and how they had themselves witnessed the Sri Lankan army treat their injuries and send them home. We only fully understood the impact of that pain when the same situation befell us in Mullivaikkal in 2009. What bell do we toll for an inquiry into the truths that were buried in the just cause of a people's freedom; from whom can we claim justice?

I was very glad when I had the chance to go back to offer help to the people affected by the tsunami. I called together some fighters and helpers and headed East. It was one of the terms of the ceasefire, that we had to have military accompaniment when we travelled through the main roads of the government-controlled areas. Those travelling in this way would have to send their name, service number, Tigers' ID card number, the time of their planned departure from the military checkpoint at Omanthai in Vavuniya, the destination and all details through the Tigers' Kilinochchi Peace Secretariat to the Colombo Peace Secretariat and leave only when they had received permission. We didn't have time for all this, so I said that we were heading to the Political Office in Vavuniya, got stamped at Omanthai and planned to drive straight through to Batticaloa. To go along with this, we took civilian clothing and dressed like ordinary women in Vavuniya. As our vehicle and the driver had government-issued papers, we were able to undertake that journey without any problems. The lorries that accompanied us had 'Tsunami Relief' signs on them, and they were able to travel behind us with no difficulties either.

When we got to the Batticaloa Political Office, we were able to meet with Political Aide Kausalyan and Brigadier Banu of the eastern province as well. They had received messages from Kilinochchi before we arrived there. The cadres there had already been engaged in relief operations. Once we had met and discussed a few things

I got ready to leave for Thirukkovil district in Amparai. The tsunami had devastated the area. I was assigned the task of serving there.

When our troop reached Thirukkoyil and Thambiluvil in Amparai, there were some helpers, including a few members of the Tamil Rehabilitation Organization, along with some cadres, in the Political Office. We made the arrangements to drop off the relief supplies in a school in Thambiluvil, close to the Political Office, where they could be secure. It was nighttime by then, and the male fighters and volunteers stayed in the school. Because there was no Women's Political Wing base in the Thirukkovil area, we could not immediately find a place to stay. The Thirukkovil area is very close to the shoreline and had suffered a terrifying amount of destruction. Even people in the areas that had not been affected had moved to other places.

We had to begin our work early the next morning, so the female cadres decided we would stay the night in the verandah of a house not far from the school, which had a well and a toilet. The cadres, who were exhausted and hungry, took turns keeping watch while the others fell into a deep sleep. We lit a small bottle lamp that we found there. Its flame flickered in the wind. The rain kept pouring endlessly. The sea, which had swallowed thousands upon thousands of lives, kept crashing with a demonic roar. When a strong wind blew, it spread a nauseating stench. I always had trouble sleeping when I felt constrained. All the events between the tsunami and that moment kept running through my mind. I wasn't sure how I would undertake relief work in a place where no one knew me. I was able to observe the tremendous damage done by the tsunami on our way here, because many Tamil homes in Amparai were situated along the shore. I had never seen the Bengal sea bubble over in black-dark waves before, and it terrified me.

The people had taken refuge in the schools, and on some small hills. That district was under government control, and there were Sri Lankan Army personnel also engaged in rescue efforts and relief efforts. We could see the army trucks show up and distribute food parcels to the people there. On another side, as the cadres and our volunteers were searching for pots to cook up the food we brought to distribute to the people, we saw some Sinhala volunteers with some of the NGOs unload some large aluminium pots. Though I did not know a word of Sinhala, I went over to them and begged them to give us some of those pots. Many who knew we were female cadres began watching us in amusement. I threw in a few English words I knew, pleaded with them, got the pots and began preparing the food right away. We loaded the cooked food into the trucks and took it to distribute to the people. In another area the army was handing out cooked food to the people as well.

The cadres distributed the clothing that had been brought in the relief trucks. The army too, had loaded clothing onto some tractors and brought them to distribute to the people. It appeared like two people in a house who were angry at each other, turning their faces away and working in competition with each other. It was no ordinary task to gather the NGOs and other organizations for a meeting, as we had in Vanni. We set up some of our cadres and volunteers in charge of some of the camps there. On one hand, the rescue work was being done by the army, the cadres, and the well-wishers of the area. The dead bodies were buried. The hardest task seemed to be to find the resources to fulfil the basic needs of the people.

Since we had set up cadres and volunteers in every camp, they were able to cook and distribute food with the people's help. Civilian teams were appointed to supervise that work. They took charge of the goods that were provided to them, stored them safely and documented them. The family details and needs of the people there were also registered. Because our cadres and volunteers were so organized, the many people and organizations that came to offer help were able to go directly to the camps and appropriately distribute the goods they had brought with the help of our crew. Many Sinhala and Muslim people and organizations also came in large numbers to undertake some aid.

The Sagamam river had overflowed its banks with the continuous rainfall. The coastal road through Thampattai was destroyed. The people urgently needed a large amount of roofing materials. Many public groups put aside ethnic and religious distinctions and offered their help. As much as we were all focused on ensuring that help reached the affected, rather than looking into who was who in those critical circumstances, there were flare-ups and arguments between our cadres and the military on many occasions. As one couldn't understand the language of the other, even the most ordinary matters could lead to huge conflicts. Regardless of whether the other person could understand what they were saying, both sides would shout at each other in their own language while they fought.

On one occasion, some female cadres had loaded up supplies in a tractor for distribution to the people staying in a small school in the Thirukkovil district. As a conflict erupted between the military who had arrived there, and our cadres, I was informed that the army had showed up in a military vehicle equipped with heavy weaponry. I was in the middle of a meeting with some NGOs at the time. When I rushed to the scene, I could see that both sides were enraged, and involved in a heated argument. When the cadres had arrived there, the army had asked them to hand over the relief supplies to them for distribution. The cadres had replied: 'These are goods we have brought. We will be distributing them; we won't be handing them over to you.' The army had countered with: 'We're going to stay here while you hand them out.' Because they couldn't understand each other clearly, the situation had escalated to the point that they had brought out heavy weaponry.

The army surrounded the place with weapons drawn. There was a university student there, who was fluent in English, and just as I asked through them if I could speak to their senior officer, the officer arrived on the scene in his vehicle. I introduced myself to him and said: 'We're here under the terms of the ceasefire agreement; impeding our work is a violation of those terms.' He asked his troop what had happened and apprised himself of the situation. Shortly after, the military official promptly sent his troops back to their base.

This official told me there would be no more obstruction to our helping the people, and he also described in detail the relief efforts the military had undertaken since the tsunami disaster had struck. He assured me that he would continue to help as much as he was able. After that, our cadres had no further trouble in distributing the goods they had brought for the civilians.

The female cadres were also involved in relief efforts in Kalmunai and Karaitivu in the Amparai district. The sight of the annihilated village called Komari still stays in my mind's eye. There were various public groups, NGOs, Tigers and army personnel engaged in relief work for Amparai and Pottuvil. They all worked according to their own schedules and didn't seem to have any intention of collaborating with each other.

I can say with conviction that if those many well-funded organizations had collaborated, learned the needs of the people, and divided up the work and acted accordingly, the people would have received far greater benefits. The Divisional Secretary of Thirukkovil, who cooperated with all sides in receiving and distributing relief supplies to the civilians was suddenly shot and killed by unknown assailants. Following that, the Political Office began receiving threatening faxes. They generally had messages like: 'Vanni Tigers get out,' 'Male or female, you will be shot indiscriminately in the street.' Under these threatening circumstances, we decided to continue helping the people while ensuring that our cadres' movements were organized with care.

It was in the eastern province that I had the most opportunities to get to know Muslim people. They interacted with us with an easy affection. It was in the East that I also got to closely observe and understand the qualities, customs and the social lives of Muslim people. It was a new experience for the cadres who had come with me as well. One time, as we crossed the Komari bridge and travelled a long distance, we sighted the temporary shelters of some Muslim people. When we got out to speak to them, the women surrounded us and talked with us, smiling and laughing the whole time. It was a joyful experience. We wanted to help these people who had suffered so many losses, and the next day we set out with some essentials to distribute to them. They included some saris, cloth and other essentials for women.

I was deeply upset when, contrary to our expectations, the women ran into their shelters when we arrived, and watched us as they hid there. The faces that had laughed and chatted with us the previous day had shadows dancing in their eyes now. One or two Muslim elders came out to speak to us. We wanted to give the things we had brought for the women to the women themselves. When we slowly peeked into their shelters and tried to speak to them, they didn't speak as freely and wholeheartedly as they had the previous day, but quietly moved away.

We asked them: 'Why aren't you talking to us the way you smiled and laughed and chatted yesterday?' 'Well, this is the edge of the street, isn't it? We don't usually come outside. Yesterday only women had come. Today, you have brought men with you,' they replied. It was very clear to us that this was just an excuse. It was obvious that someone had forbidden them to talk to us. Even after we talked to them, they only accepted the supplies we had brought for them with some hesitation. Yet, they and our female cadres had genuinely wanted to get to know each other as friends. They had brought out food and tea they had made in their shelters and shared it with us and showed us great hospitality. When I think back on those delightful minutes when they had sat close to us and held our hands, laughing and talking all the while, my eyes cloud over with tears. The last days of Mullivaikkal brought home to me how many loving paths we had closed off and how we had isolated ourselves to protect our armed struggle.

It was only when I spent time in the eastern province that I grasped the importance of learning from an early age to interact with people of different natures and traditions, and to grow up with a deep understanding of their feelings. My own experiences have taught me that though this wide, expansive world may hold many divisions and differences, humanity's shared language of love is the bridge that can overcome all obstacles and connect humankind. As much as there is justice in our desire to protect the traditions of our people, and live true to ourselves, it is also vital that we understand and respect the rights and sensibilities of other groups. I believe that the chauvinism and dishonesty of the older generations who determined the course of political history in the island of Sri Lanka have destroyed the lives of an entire generation.

During the tsunami relief operations, I had the chance to serve together with Tamil youth, male and female, Muslims, Sinhalese and all manner of people. The remarkable strength of collective spirit that was revealed there overwhelmed and amazed me. The heads of the Sri Lankan government channelled all that creative energy into the war and destroyed it in the war.

We had also organized some performances to try and give the people some relief from the emotional damage inflicted by the loss of their relatives and possessions in the disaster. The schoolteachers and students got together to organize these events in the temporary shelters created for the people. It was a kind of balm to the people's wounded hearts. Usually, when there is a death, the village shows up to comfort the bereaved family. When the whole village was reeling with death, the mothers who had lost their children sat numbly, barely able to open their mouths to cry.

We thought that if they let out their grief through crying and wailing, there might be some hope of easing their mental anguish, and so we organized a memorial event a month after the tsunami. Representatives from the various groups participating in tsunami relief were also invited to that event. I had invited the army commander of the Thirukkovil district to light the first flame on the memorial lamp. He accepted my request with no hesitation and lit the lamp. Following that, the people lit candles and remembered their relatives. A couple of the representatives and I delivered eulogies to comfort the people. For the first time, we had joined with the Sri Lankan military and carried out an important event to provide solace to the people.

There was a meeting organized in Vanni to discuss continued tsunami relief, and I was required to attend. I set off with a couple of female cadres, after setting my work in order in the east. Kausalyan, the political chief of Batticaloa district, had also been summoned to the meeting, and I set off from Thirukkovil, while he set off from Batticaloa. The meeting for the leaders took place at the Political Secretariat in Kilinochchi at around nine the next morning. As it was the first meeting for the political leaders after the tsunami disaster, a number of important issues were brought up. We finished the meeting and were ready to head back east that evening. We thought that if we travelled through the night, we'd be able to resume our work the next morning. The vehicle Kausalyan was in drove just ahead of mine, and we passed the military checkpoint at Vavuniya and travelled along the A9 highway.

Kausalyan's vehicle stopped in front of a lodge in Polonnaruwa town and he called me on the radio, saying 'Akka come, let's eat something and head out.' My cadres and I had eaten lunch before we started out. We had the water bottles and packets of biscuits we might need for the trip in the vehicle as well. When we had to go on long journeys like this, we never stopped the vehicles or delayed along the way unless it was absolutely necessary. Since female combatants were easier to identify than male combatants, I tended to be extremely careful when we travelled through government-controlled areas. So, I told him that we had already eaten, and that we'd go on ahead. 'You eat and come,' I said. Our vehicle kept going.

Kausalyan was heading to Batticaloa, and I was heading to Thirukkovil. Our vehicle was travelling on the Mahiyanganai road to Amparai. Kausalyan did not contact me after that; I didn't contact him either. It must have been past ten at night, I think. Suddenly, a call came through from the Political Aide's main communication centre.

'Thamizhini akka, have you run into any trouble?'

'We're not having any trouble. Why do you ask?' I said. They replied, 'One of the vehicles that set out from Kilinochchi was hit today, so we called to check on you. Stay in touch, we'll contact you shortly.'

The memory of last separating from Kausalyan's vehicle in Polonnaruwa came to my mind. I immediately tried to establish contact with Kausalyan. The call went out; no one replied. I realized Kausalyan must have run into trouble. A short while later, the call came in from Kilinochchi.

'It was Kausalyan's vehicle that was hit on Welikanda road; no one survived, the MP for Amparai, Chandranehru was also in the vehicle. He's gone too.'

It pained me deeply that the fighters who had accompanied us from Kilinochchi were dead even before we reached our destination. Kausalyan was the kind of fighter who approached people with easy friendship and affection. He had been the Treasurer of the Batticaloa district and was later made a Political officer. Whenever he came to Kilinochchi, he would come by our base and tell us all about the projects undertaken by the female cadres in Batticaloa before he left.

During the women's conference that was held in Batticaloa, he introduced me to the woman he hoped to marry. After they married, they had come to our Kilinochchi base. Kausalyan and his wife, who had a degree from the Eastern University, were a couple very much in love. When Kausalyan lost his life, his wife was pregnant. My heart sank thinking of her condition when she received the news of his death. In the fight for our rights, every fighter had to cope with many thousands of events like this. Yet, it is difficult to bear the pain they cause.

When we were in Thirukkovil in Amparai working as part of the tsunami relief effort, Member of Parliament Hon. Chandranehru had helped us out a lot. He was held in the very highest esteem by the people of that district. You could see that his family had been in politics from the time of Thanthai Chelva.

The last rites for all those who died with him were observed in massive memorial events. The Political Aide arrived from the Peace Secretariat by helicopter to participate in the funeral rites.

After the attack on Kausalyan, it was terrifying for the fighters to keep up with the relief work openly. The tsunami relief projects began to dwindle. People whose houses had not been damaged returned to their homes. Temporary shelters made of tin roofing were constructed for people who had lost their entire homes. Beyond that, road building and electricity supply was undertaken by the relevant departments. I formed a team of women from the Political Wing to continue working in Amparai. We selected the village of Thangavelayuthapuram and organized a two-day village base there, to give them an experience and to do some foundational work for a village that was very underdeveloped.

That village served as a site for the Chena cultivation needs of the people from Thirukkovil, Thambiluvil and Vinayakapuram districts. There was just a small shop and a small school there. The school principal told us that the children tended to come to school only when there was no work on the farms. The village folks had to walk through the fields quite far from the main road. We went house to house to meet the people who had camped out at the school for two days. The crops were lush and beautiful to look at. They farmed a variety of crops, including yams, great millet, sorghum, finger millet and vegetables. Without the aid of artificial fertilizers, these crops grew profusely in the natural strength of the soil.

Three female cadres who were working in the Karaitivu and Kalmunai areas informed me that they were coming to meet me in Thirukkovil. We had returned to our base after finishing up our work in Thangavelayuthapuram. Many of the cadres had gone out to do their work. Our vehicle had gone to Akkaraipattu to drop off the teachers who had been invited to our 'village base' event and was on its way back. Because we were living under threat at that time, we had to take several precautions and warn the cadres before they were sent out.

Shortly after, a boy came running to our base and delivered an urgent message to us. 'Three akkas from the Movement have been shot by someone on the Thampattai road; they have been taken to the Thirukkovil hospital now.'

I quickly jumped on a cycle lying around the base and sped off to the hospital. Only one of the fighters was conscious and able to speak. They had put her in an ambulance to take her to Akkaraipattu hospital.

They had been in an auto, on their way to Thirukkovil, when a young man on a bicycle had called out 'Thamizhini akka'. One of the cadres in the auto had a name that also began with 'Thamizh'. Thinking that someone was calling out to her, she had asked the auto to stop. As the auto slowed down, the young man had taken out a gun from his bag and fired a volley of shots at them. The cadre in charge of the group had received more than three bullets to the chest. The auto driver had run away in fear. It was not a busy street, and some civilians passing by had put the women into a vehicle and brought them to the hospital.

They were admitted to Akkaraipattu hospital, and the staff immediately said they needed blood transfusions. Even before our cadres from the Thirukkovil area could get to the hospital, some of the youth from Akkaraipattu had donated blood to save the cadres. Their condition was critical and, because we couldn't guarantee their safety, I sent an urgent message to the Political Aide that we needed to move them to a different location and waited for a reply.

As we were under a ceasefire agreement, it was decided in accordance with the measures taken by the Peace Secretariat, that they would be moved to Colombo with the government's assistance. They were taken to Colombo for further medical treatment, in an Avro airplane belonging to the Sri Lankan Air Force that had been arranged for the purpose. If those emergency measures had not been taken, those cadres would not have survived.

The people I met, and the places I saw when I went to Thirukkovil district for tsunami relief work, and the opportunity the work gave me to get to know Sinhalese and Muslim people, were all experiences that created a profound impact on me. I would like to record here that those experiences also created significant changes in my political perspective.

I had also gone to Trincomalee during a propaganda trip to the eastern province in 2004. Brigadier Sornam was in charge there at the time. When I visited a number of villages near the Trincomalee town and the Tiger-controlled area of Sampur, the sight of three- and four-year-old children breaking rocks in the Ilakanthai area, and the atrocious conditions of the even more backward villages including Santhosapuram and Malaimunthal imprinted some unbearably sad sights in my mind.

Our female cadres had organized a meeting with the people of a backward village. I don't properly recall the name of the village. The majority in that village were beggars by occupation. Our fighters had gone early and stopped the people from leaving and kept them there. When we went for the meeting, I noticed that the people's fingers, from the elderly to the children, seemed different in some way. Their fingers had developed sores and seemed worn away. I took pictures of this phenomenon with a camera I had with me. When I asked them, they said it was 'diabetes/sugar disease.' When there was a Public Health Department meeting held in Trincomalee town, I had the opportunity of attending it, and I showed them the pictures I had taken and gave them the details of the village I had visited. The doctors who examined the photos noted that it was a form of leprosy. Our team was called back to Vanni the very next day. I never got to know what medical assistance was organized for that village after that.

The cost the eastern province, so abundant in natural resources, has paid towards the armed struggle and cannot be underestimated by anyone. Each of its people has many sorrowful stories to tell. The stories of their children: their flesh, blood and life-pulse, are the most common of those stories. I bow my head eternally to the memory of the relationships with those who called me 'daughter, daughter' and showered me with love.

7

A False Peace and Disrupted Civilian Life

When the Liberation Tigers and the Sri Lankan government signed a ceasefire agreement in February of 2002, political analysts were amazed to see the events organized in Kilinochchi, which was now on par with Colombo as a political capital. The first phase was the arrival of our political strategist Anton Balasingham and his wife from England to the Maldives; from there they flew via a rented Maldives Air taxi and disembarked at the Iranamadu tank. The Leader Prabhakaran, his wife Mathivathani, and several important delegates, colonels and officers of the Movement had arrived to greet them. I too went, along with women Brigadiers Vithusha and Thurka. There was happiness and excitement in everybody's faces that day. The Leader had set aside his usual camouflage uniform for a pale blue 'safari' suit that had been tailored for him. It filled everyone's hearts with a sense of peace and confidence seeing him laugh and talk in a relaxed manner.

A small amphibious aircraft, with a light engine, flew over Kilinochchi, slowly circled Iranamadu tank, landed on the expanse of water, and glided a short distance before coming to a stop. The special team of Sea Tigers had already identified a suitable landing area for the seaplane and marked it with buoys.

Political Aide Thamilselvan, Sea Tigers Special Colonel Soosai and Treasury Officer Thamizhenthi went out in an inflatable plastic raft and received Anton Balasingham and his wife, and brought them in. The experienced Sea Tiger cadres were very careful in steering the raft back. Anton Balasingham suffered from a life-threatening kidney ailment. He had undertaken a perilous sea journey when he left the country and undergone surgery before returning to negotiate in the peace talks. When Anton Balasingham arrived at Iranamadu tank, leader Prabhakaran held his arm and helped him disembark from the raft.

The atmosphere was that of a family reunited after a long time, and the air was full of questions about each other's health and wellbeing. Everyone there already knew Anton Balasingham and his wife and enjoyed some closeness with them. They both had the remarkable ability to remember a fighter they had only met once and pat them on the shoulder and ask how they were doing; many ordinary cadres loved them a great deal.

I met Anton Balasingham and his wife Adele for the first time in Jaffna in 1993, in their home. At the time I had written a political essay for the 'Freedom Birds' magazine. I had told my friend Malaimakal that I wanted to show it to one of the elders and get some feedback on it. It was she who took me to Anton Balasingham's home for the first time. As he already knew Malaimakal, he asked me my name. At the time, my name was Chandrika. When he heard the name, a smile spread across his face. 'Hm…Madame Chandrika, what's happening? What work are you doing?' he asked. I felt a little nervous that I was speaking to an important figure in the Movement; someone I had only known through the media till that moment. His wife brought us some delicious tea and sat smiling next to us. 'Have you eaten? What did you have?' she asked. I was surprised to observe a white woman attempt to speak the Tamil language as best she could and pronounce it so beautifully.

Mr. Balasingham said: 'Read it out loud, child' when I gave him the essay. I read it. After listening to the whole thing with his eyes closed, 'Cut this paragraph, think through this paragraph well and rewrite it. Not bad. This is how you should keep practising and learn to write. Clever girl! Read as many books as you can. To write even a little, you must read a lot. What is it, I say? Do you understand what I mean?' he countered in his usual style. I nodded my head quickly. I can say that the female cadres interacted with Anton and Adele Balasingham with a sense of entitled familiarity. Though Adele was a white woman, she was humble, and related easily with everyone.

As the first phase in the cessation of hostilities, the Peace Secretariat was set up in Kilinochchi. The roads were opened again. The Tiger leadership entered the political arena right away, with intense enthusiasm, and one of the things they did was hold an international media conference in Kilinochchi and meet with Muslim and hill country politicians as well as various other politicians. Though the Movement claimed the migration from Jaffna was a tactical retreat, it was in fact the greatest defeat the Tigers had ever faced. However, now the Tigers were full of triumph that it was their continued victories during the ferocious battles of Vanni, following this defeat, that had brought about a shift in our political circumstances. The Tigers' Movement, which had now gained a reputation as a strong military and political force in the country of Sri Lanka, was determined that it should take full advantage of its bargaining power in the peace talks undertaken with international mediators.

Political Aide Thamilselvan shared leader Prabhakaran's words after signing the ceasefire agreement in 2002 with the other commanders. 'Anna said, "I've put my signature to it, but the real problems are yet to come. We must increase our troops, and clearly put forward to the people the need for cadres in government-controlled areas, to recruit young men and women for the Movement." We must use this interval to work frantically and increase our troop strength. In the early days we had no weapons, but we had manpower. Now the Movement has all the weapons as we need. But not enough troops. We must assemble those troops. You need to move in the knowledge that the peace talks are for the outside world alone, they don't apply to us,' he said.

Though the ceasefire agreement between the Sri Lankan government and the Tigers gave the people some respite and comfort after a protracted war, it didn't reassure them of a lasting peace. The people understood only too well, from past experiences, that both sides, the government and the Tigers, would not enter wholeheartedly into any peace process. So, they used these intervals as and when they occurred, to ameliorate their disordered lives to some extent. The people rebuilt the houses and shops destroyed by the protracted war, entirely by their own efforts. Watching the peace process, the prevailing mood among the people seemed to be pessimistic: 'When are you going to start again?' 'Let us know before you start,' 'If we build a structure to withstand another five years that should do.'

Peace talks were conducted in the major political and economic capitals of Bangkok, Geneva and Tokyo. The Tigers had intended that the peace talks be conducted in two phases. First, they wanted to address the everyday concerns of the civilians and reach some agreement they could put into practice. The Tigers were determined that the peace talks could then shift to the vital phase of discussing basic political issues. However, even while discussing the concerns of civilians, the government pushed for a political decision to be reached or abandoned. It was at that time that chief spokesperson Anton Balasingham put forward the idea that an ad hoc interim judicial process be created. The Western world and the Sri Lankan government latched onto these conciliatory gestures on the part of the Tigers and began a stratagem to bring the Tigers in line. Sensing that political control was slipping out of his hands and snaring him in a blockade of international diplomacy the Leader, with his usual rigidity, moved towards decisions that displeased the Sri Lankan government and the Western world. The note of peace slowly slid out of tune.

Norway came forward to negotiate peace terms with the support of the international community in response to the Tigers' request for a third attempt at negotiating peace talks with the Sri Lankan government. A Security Council for the cessation of war was formed under Western delegates. The international community that operated in this manner in the third phase, put into practice their own modern techniques and set up their own programmes, with the intention of carrying out successful peace talks built on a foundation of diplomacy. That is, not only were they aiming to negotiate between both sides involved in the war, meet their terms, preside at the conference table and act as mediators, they were also willing to do work among the civilians on both sides of the war, to bring about some reconciliation. They attempted to create commercial relationships between the Sinhala, Tamil and Muslim communities, communication between feminist organizations, and educational resources for students. They also planned various ways to bring together the separated communities, with the intention of redressing the impact of the conflict and convincing all parties of the urgency of a peaceful solution.

Once the highways were opened up again, many international NGOs began to enter the Tamil areas with their new projects. Even hearing the titles of their projects, like 'Rebuilding Peace', 'Reconciliation Between Ethnic Groups' and so on became unbearably annoying for the Tigers. As a result, the Tigers did not like the NGOs working directly with the civilian population. They decided that the NGOs could only work with the population under the guidance of the Administrative Centre established by the Tigers in Kilinochchi. The Administrative Centre in Kilinochchi had already gathered and readied details of affected civilians, needs assessments, and project plans for work to be done for the civilian population. The Tigers had absolutely no wish to have outsiders gather personal data or mingle among the people to discuss their needs. The people watched bemused as the various NGOs, bearing new names that were hard to comprehend, came in rows of vehicles with their various coloured flags flying up the A9 in the early days. However, they were unable to withstand the stipulations the Tigers put on their activities and many organizations fled with their dignity in shreds.

Some organizations came forward with the idea of building permanent housing for the people who had lost their homes during the war, but they were informed that they had to build the houses according to the specifications of the Tigers. I was also involved in consultations with them. As the North is a very arid zone, ordinary tin sheet roofing could not be used for the roofs for permanent housing. We could not use asbestos sheets either, as they are said to be hazardous to human health. The Tigers suggested that they needed durable roofing materials that could provide cooling, or such materials should be researched.

At the same meeting, we put forward a suggestion on behalf of the Women's Front. Since women used the house the most, specific amenities needed to be included that took women and children into account. Accordingly, the kitchens needed to be well ventilated, a chimney needed to be added to vent smoke from the house, a small sheltered porch needed to be set up where children coming home from school could rest if the adults had locked up the house and were not in when they got back. Many women in the areas where they still used wood fires for cooking, told us of the respiratory ailments they suffered as a result of constantly inhaling smoke. Many of the organizations that accepted our suggestions, built homes according to these specifications.

In 2003, as a means of strengthening the peace talks, women delegates from the Sri Lankan Government and from the Tigers met in the Peace Secretariat in Kilinochchi under the mediation of Norway. Five government delegates, including two Muslim women, participated in the talks. Their chief speaker was Prof. Kumari Jayawardene. She is an experienced social researcher and has published many research books as well. All those who worked with her were experts in the fields of feminism, social sciences, law and medicine. I was appointed chief speaker representing the LTTE. Four cadres who had worked with me in the Political Wing were also involved. They had experiences arising from having worked for a long time with the women in our society. They were also chosen to represent Batticaloa and Trincomalee districts. The mediator for this meeting was the former Member of Parliament in Norway, and a social science and psychology expert, Hon. Astrid Heiberg.

The LTTE's political strategist Anton Balasingham prepared us for this meeting. He informed us that these adjunct meetings held great importance in the advancement of the peace talks. These meetings were arranged between women delegates building on the premise that during the prolonged war in Sri Lanka it is women on both sides who had suffered the most losses and hardships, and that their inquiries and the decisions they reached on the special needs of women would inform projects undertaken in the future. When needed, the women delegates would also be included in the peace talks, he informed us.

'The women delegates coming from the South are very well educated. They are all academics. That doesn't mean you should worry; you have the experience of having witnessed firsthand the problems of women living under wartime conditions. I have faith in you; you are untutored experts,' he said as he encouraged us. At the time we asked him to clarify some of our concerns as well. The most important of these concerned the mass killings. The largest number of casualties in the mass killings in the eastern province and the aerial bombardments of civilians were women and children; our cadres were of the opinion that we should address some of these matters in those meetings as well, but when we told him about this, he wouldn't allow it, and gave the following explanation.

'Don't think that they are the only ones who have committed mass killings. The Tigers are not entirely saints either. If we give them a list of mass killings, they will come with a list of the mass killings committed by the Tigers as well. So, digging up these matters now will only complicate things for both sides,' he said.

'It is a good thing to do some research into improving women's lives. It will be very useful for you to share your experiences with them, and for them to share their experiences with you; your projects will definitely come to the negotiating table in the future. Today, it is the rights of women that are coming to the forefront. Until now, there have not been any such meetings during the talks. This is a precious opportunity; you must use this opportunity well and create an environment where development projects that will improve the lives of those affected, especially the women, will happen.' He brought up many rationales as he prepared us.

The government delegates arrived in a Sri Lankan air force helicopter at the Kilinochchi stadium grounds. The Norwegian mediators, who had arrived by land, were staying at the Rangeview Hotel near Kilinochchi lake. At around 10 am, for the first time in history, women delegates on behalf the government and the LTTE met under the facilitation of Norwegian mediators. After the preliminary introductions, some important issues were addressed under the chairpersonship of the mediator. I spoke of the issues facing Tamil women who had been affected by the war, on behalf of the LTTE. I put forward some brief points about the affected women as well. Kumari Jayawardene, who had come as chief spokesperson of the Sri Lankan government, said: 'Beyond ethnicity and religion, we are women. It is women who have experienced the greatest sufferings in this country as a result of the war, and so, during these peace talks we must come together to talk about what must be done for women,' and she put forward her own points. After that, the meeting continued until the afternoon. They brought up the tribulations faced by Sinhalese women who had lost their husbands during the war; the families who were in search of their soldier husbands who had gone missing during the war; and the Sinhala families displaced from the border villages during the LTTE attacks, and their struggles to find a livelihood. It was finally decided that a Women's Peace Secretariat needed to be established, and that could be used as a base to mobilize the women's projects to the next stages.

When it was suggested that the main office of the Women's Peace Secretariat be established in Colombo, and the adjunct office be set up in Kilinochchi, we completely refused, and gave them the reasoning behind our objection. 'It is true that women on both sides have been affected by the war. At the same time, when you draw a comparison, it is in the north and east that women have been affected the most, and the most work needs to be undertaken in these areas. Therefore, it makes more sense to have the headquarters of the Women's Peace Secretariat in Kilinochchi.' Our logic was accepted. At the end of our meeting that day, we released a joint statement to the press.

Meeting

These meetings took place twice in Kilinochchi. During the second meeting, a programme was drawn up as to how the Women's Peace Secretariat would be run. As Norway had agreed to provide the resources needed to run the Secretariat, a budget was drawn up to run it as well. In that environment of uncertainty as to how long the peace talks would last, I didn't really have much faith that the women's meetings would realistically accomplish much. Yet it was an unusual experience for me to have the chance to speak so openly with women from other societies about the condition of Tamil women and, beyond politics, to hear the opinions of diverse women who were of the same opinions when it came to the issues facing women in wartime. After the meetings, I felt a deep affinity with them, and the strengthening of a unique friendship, far more than our differences of opinion. Thinking back, in the later days, I felt that if only women had been allowed to participate more in the talks between the different groups, there could have been far greater opportunities for social progress. In the days following these meetings, when the Norwegian delegates approached us with the intention of handing over the funds to support the establishment of a Women's Peace Secretariat, the leadership of the Movement had decided to back away from the peace talks. They refused to accept the money and sent it back.

Though there were many incidents in the beginning that came close to terminating the peace talks, peace somehow escaped with its life by a hair's breadth. I saw such an incident within the first day or two of the talks.

Anton Balasingham was preparing to leave for London, after having stayed a few days in Vanni and attending several important meetings. Several of the higher-ups had come to his house to see him off in a helicopter. I was there as well. The Leader Prabhakaran arrived there shortly after. As he was happily talking to Anton Balasingham, Colonel Soosai of the Black Tigers arrived there in agitated state. As soon as he arrived, he rushed to where the Leader and Anton Balasingham were speaking and spoke urgently to them. Soon they all began talking in heated tones. The Tigers' radar station had picked up some movement of the Sri Lankan Navy's 'Dvora' high-speed patrol boats in the deep-sea area of

Mullaitivu. Colonel Soosai had prepared the Sea Tigers for attack and had come with the intention of apprising the Leader of the situation right away and getting permission to strike.

Anton Balasingham asked him to stay calm for a while, and immediately called Pulithevan, who was functioning as Peace Secretary. He asked the latter to establish urgent communications with the Colombo Peace Secretariat and the Ceasefire Monitoring Committee, and once this had been done, spoke with them. Balasingham told the Leader that the Sri Lankan government had established communication with the relevant people and were restraining the movements of the military vessels. For a few hours, that place was under high pressure. Colonel Soosai kept receiving updates on the movements of the 'Dvora' boats. Anton Balasingham stayed on the line with the head of the Ceasefire Monitoring Committee. Soosai kept threatening to act: 'Bala anna! Even now the Dvora boatmen are moving around. If they come close to the shore, tell them we'll strike!' 'Wait a little longer. The head of the Ceasefire Monitoring Committee is talking to the Naval Commander right now, they'll tell us the decision,' Anton Balasingham replied, shaking like an ant trapped by fire on either side.

A short while later, Colonel Soosai received news that the Sri Lankan Navy's 'Dvora' boats had disappeared from the Tiger radar screens. He ordered the Sea Tiger attack forces to return to their bases. The Leader, who was lost in thought, his face grim up to then, began laughing and joking with everyone there in his usual manner. Everyone who had been watching the goings on as if it were a movie, heaved a tremendous sigh of relief. If there had been any delays, the entire situation would have turned on its head. Everyone there knew that the Leader would have given Colonel Soosai permission to attack. Because Prabhakaran remained an immensely powerful man who could decide whether there would be war or peace on the island of Sri Lanka.

As the measures for peace crept along at tortoise pace, there were many changes made within the internal structure of the Movement. The most important of these was regarding the Movement's troop strength. The taproot of the Movement lay there. That began to waver, little by little. When Karuna, who was Colonel in the eastern province, announced that he wished to separate from the Movement, it sent shockwaves through the LTTE, even though none of this was visible from the outside. Karuna Amman was the most highly regarded, top ranking Colonel in the Movement. There were many highly skilled combatants and junior Colonels with him. There was no denying that they had proven their strength in the battlegrounds of Vanni. As a result, half the Movement's military strength was lost once Karuna Amman went his own way.

When Karuna Amman separated from the Movement in April of 2004, I was in Jaffna, helping with campaign work for the parliamentary elections that were to happen that month. The Tigers believed that if they created a Tamil political party, and campaigned for its victory in the elections, they could demonstrate that the Tamil people were behind them, and they could also establish their influence in parliamentary decisions. At the time Ilamparathi was the Political Officer of Jaffna district. I was one of the cadres sent from Vanni to help him. I don't remember what day it was, when Ilamparathi called an urgent secret meeting for the fighters.

'An important message has come in from Kilinochchi, which I have to share with you. The Batticaloa-Amparai Colonel has stated that he is separating from the Movement, along with his six thousand fighters,' Ilamparathi broke the news to the fighters who were present.

Everyone sat stunned and motionless. After hearing this news, nothing else that was said there seemed to register in my ears. I felt in that minute that the whole Movement had been destroyed. The eastern province fighters held such a strong position in the army of the Liberation Tigers' Movement. We had been asked to halt all public election gatherings until we received further word from Kilinochchi. We stayed huddled in our bases in Potpathy road in Kokuvil, for two whole days, unable to do anything. Neither were we able to face the volley of questions from the people.

We were in a confused state, with no idea of how to respond to the people. We were called to a meeting of the heads of the Political Wing the next day. We were told at the meeting that when the

Batticaloa-Amparai Colonel was called in for an inquiry concerning misappropriation of funds and a personal disciplinary issue, he had refused to come in, and made this announcement. As a result, he was now removed from the Liberation Tigers' Movement, and the Movement was now engaged in measures to liberate the cadres being held by him. The Political Aide told us that the fighters need not be upset by this; our leader Prabhakaran had successfully overcome many such crises before and he would overcome this one as well; we could clearly, confidently respond to the people's questions.

At that time, the memories of Mahattaya anna, who had been deputy leader of the Movement, and then arrested and executed, came to mind. If the Movement had decided that this was to be someone's punishment, the charges brought against them were invariably that they conspired against the Leader, they misappropriated Movement funds, or that they committed sex crimes. I also knew that when the other liberation Movements were quashed, similar accusations were made against them. What had really transpired between the Leader and the Colonel of the eastern province remained an utter mystery to me and many of the other fighters. However, I can firmly say to some extent that leader Prabhakaran had immeasurable confidence in him and a special affection for him.

One day Colonels Vithusha, Thurka and I were called to meet with the Leader. This was in the early stages of the Peace Talks. The Leader was speaking to us about many matters. At one point, he said: 'The fighters from Batticaloa and Amparai have undergone so many difficulties in the struggle. We must give them a lot of help—and the civilians there. I have arranged for some money through the treasury, and I have told Karuna as well to give those people a lot of help. He's doing it, but Pottu's men keep coming to me saying "that is wrong, this is wrong"; first there needs to be some unity between the Colonels.'

After the conflict between Colonel Karuna of Batticaloa-Amparai, and the LTTE, some fighters came over to Vanni out of their faith in the Tiger leadership. They too were enlisted, as a terrible internecine war, 'brother against brother', began; it was titled 'Actions to Redeem the Fighters in the Eastern Province'.

Cadres whom I had known for many years died on both sides of that battle. Four female fighters, including Colonel Sapthahiki (Charlie) and many male Colonels who had surrendered in good faith to the Tigers, were confined to the cells of the Movement's Intelligence Division, and we heard they had received a death sentence. The Movement's military strength began to wither under these kinds of brutal measures.

Many of the longest serving fighters of the LTTE had suffered serious injuries in the wars. With that, some junior officers too began to leave the Movement, citing personal reasons. To my knowledge, many male and female fighters left the Movement because of their families' poverty, or because their parents forced them to. Many others left because of their romantic relationships or when they got married. As a result, the numbers of experienced fighters in the attack squads kept dwindling.

After 30 years of war, we were left with injured and aging fighters who could not undergo rigorous training. They had spent and lost their youth and their physical strength in the service of freedom for the nation. Many seriously injured male and female fighters who were no longer in active service, clung to life in the hope and faith that 'no matter who abandons us, anna will not abandon us'. Even if we found it hard sometimes to reconcile ourselves to some of the work we were commanded to do by the Movement, many officers and cadres would say the same words: 'If anna says so, we must do it, mustn't we?' and 'Anna must have some plan for all this'.

Many criticized this as devotion to a single man. There's truth to that. I believe this is a trait that comes with our traditions and customs. Thousands of fighters like myself saw the Leader as someone who had put a face to so many crises and had nurtured a revolution of more than 30 years through great military strength. In those instances when the decisions the Leader made came under any kind of criticism, each fighter believed with the utmost conviction that he made those decisions for the good of the people and for the freedom of our nation, and that there would be some reasoning behind the decisions he made. Within the Movement, criticizing the Leader's decisions, or questioning them, was considered almost a religious taboo. The growth of this practice, which eventually erased any criticism or debate within the Movement, also paved the way for its utter destruction.

From the high-ranking brigadiers of the attack troops, the commanding colonels and field officers to the ordinary cadres, we were trained to follow the military chain of command and obey the orders of the Movement's leadership. The leadership we were aware of, in a general sense, were senior, important leaders like Anton Balasingham, former head of EROS Balakumaran, Treasury Officer Thamizhenthy and Senior Brigadier and Chief Intelligence Officer Pottu Amman. Of these, only Anton Balasingham could voice his opinions to the Leader with some authority.

In the final peace talks, Anton Balasingham was determined to reach an agreement on a Federal Government model and suggested that he was prepared to put forward a decision on 'internal self-determination'. However, that model was not palatable to Leader Prabhakaran. He accused the international powers of planning to seize the Tigers' arms from them under the guise of agreeing to a political decision. He believed that Anton Balasingham had also been ensnared in their net. The Leader was not going to allow his weapons to leave his hands for even a fraction of a moment, as long as he was alive. As a result, the two became embroiled in a bitter argument, to the point that they could no longer bear to look at each other. Anton Balasingham finally left Kilinochchi a heartbroken man. The usual smiles and laughter had disappeared when they got into their helicopter to leave, and many of us noticed tears brimming in his and his wife's eyes.

The Liberation Tigers split into their divisions and began their organizational work among the people, but there were no conditions to create a unifying organization to oversee the divisional activities even to the end. The divisional heads kept going with the intention that it would suffice if their division simply did their own work well. In keeping with the Leader's suggestion, the colonels and chief officers met on a monthly basis to compile and address the concerns that arose among the people and reach some ad hoc agreement on organizational issues.

While this helped address some basic issues, it was not possible to effect any overall change. The manner in which the Liberation Tigers' collected their tax came under severe criticism from the people. Some of the people accused the Tigers of extorting money from a civilian population that had already been economically devastated by a protracted war. No matter what explanation Treasurer Thamizhenthy gave the people, they would not accept it wholeheartedly. Beyond this, the deficiencies in the approach of the officers who worked among them exacerbated the problems. When their relatives came from overseas on holiday visits during peace time, they too sharply pointed out the deficiencies. There was a huge signboard in Omanthai, at the point where the Tiger-controlled area began, stating: 'The Soil of Vanni Welcomes You'. The people resented the Movement's taxation practice so much that they began to ridicule the sign with a play on words, saying 'The Soil of Vanni Makes You Sweat'.

Another issue that created conflict between the people and the Movement, was forced conscription. There had been no direct communication between the people who were in the government-controlled areas and the Tigers, and when they first saw the Tigers they came as a wave of young men and women and enlisted as recruits. But as the days went by, that wave began to lose its momentum. As a result, it became necessary to take up intensive propaganda efforts in the government-controlled areas as well. New training bases for male and female fighters were set up during peace times, and basic combat training continued. Along with that, training for border patrol forces and auxiliary forces were also resumed. A plan was also put in place to bring back the fighters who had left the Movement. With this, the people were subjected to many pressures. The Movement's actions began to shift very, very gradually from recruitment through propaganda to forced conscription.

The Movement had reached a terrible state where the notion that it was acceptable to get anyone, by any means, to join up as a member had begun to take hold. The principles of the Movement

Thamizhini with other fighters

began to shrink to the point that it was enough for us merely to have bodies that could be trained to carry and fire weapons. Under the guise of political service, the Movement's various divisions were plunged full force into this project.

In the history of this war of more than 30 years, thousands of fighters had sacrificed their lives, and tens of thousands of people had lost their lives and possessions and suffered unbearable anguish. Yet, because of the victories the Tigers had had in battle, and because of their children, who had sacrificed their lives, the people bore up with the shortcomings and trespasses of the Tigers and the many pains and burdens of armed conflict with equanimity. In spite of all their criticisms, they believed that the Liberation Tigers who had risen as the single political force of the Tamil people would somehow prove to be their saviours and win them their freedom.

After the tsunami struck in December of 2004, talks began with countries willing to offer international aid to bring together the Sri Lankan government with the Tigers for rebuilding projects, under the Post-Tsunami Operational Management Structure. However, the Tigers could not engage in these talks with much faith. Without any legal authority being given to the Tigers to undertake these projects, giving permission to the Sri Lankan government to start rebuilding in Tamil areas was a problem for the Tigers. With the unprecedented situation of the Tamil people's political struggle being managed with the arbitration of the Western world, the Tigers' leadership needed a kind of diplomatic initiative to engage in the ensuing political situation.

Our leader Prabhakaran, who had baffled the Sri Lankan armed forces and international military researchers with his military prowess in the battlefield and won so many victories, began to stumble when it came to employing the nuanced skills of diplomacy during a time of peace, which was needed to move the Tamil people towards a firm political solution. He was in a situation where he now had to put aside his headstrong nature for the sake of the people who still believed in the struggle, even when they had lost all form of sustenance. But, he did not seem to have the confidence to make that shift. The question of whether he should safeguard the very people he was fighting for, or whether he should safeguard the weapons he had gathered at the expense of millions of lives, and in the midst of extreme difficulties, rose before him in the form of flesh and blood.

The peace talks appeared unable to proceed beyond a point and began to harden. While the SIRHN (Sub-committee for Immediate Rehabilitation and Humanitarian Needs) was set up with the consent of the LTTE, with the intention of undertaking development projects for civilians affected by the war, the LTTE began to openly object to some of its activities. The Norwegian mediators were engaged in heightened efforts to take the LTTE to a conference in New York with countries willing to offer aid. Airline seats were reserved for the Tigers' delegates until the last minute. Among the LTTE, there was some ambivalence towards the end about whether they would attend or not. At the last minute, we heard that the Leader had made the final decision not to go.

During a meeting at the Peace Secretariat, Political Aide Thamilselvan said to us: 'Anna believes that if we go to this conference, we'll become entrapped in an international net. America and other Western countries have only come down so far to talk to us with the intent of seizing our weapons. But anna says there is no room for a debate on surrendering our arms. What else, now?

It's going to be war. Anna says you must drop all your other work and recruit fighters for the Movement. The battle we are facing now is not just with the Sri Lankan Armed Forces, but an international war. You and I need not worry ourselves too much about that. Anna will handle it. If we each of us do the work as he asks, he will take care of when and what decisions have to be made.'

From the end of 2004, there were increasing violations of the ceasefire agreement between the armed forces and the Tigers. The Ceasefire Monitoring Committee kept documenting these crimes and sending their reports to the Peace Secretariats on either side. On 12 August 2005, the Sri Lankan Minister for Foreign Affairs, Lakshman Kadirgamar, was felled by an LTTE sniper attack. The next day, at a meeting of the Officers, Leader Prabhakaran, who was at the event remarked: 'Well, they kept scratching and scratching away. We've hit them where it hurts.'

The strike had taken place in a highly secure location in Sri Lanka and demonstrated the Tigers' ability to attack. When the fourth phase of the Eelam War began, the LTTE's colonels were convinced that the war would take place outside the north and east. The Movement also believed that the LTTE Intelligence Division had successfully penetrated the government-controlled areas as well with that intent. In addition, the strength of the air force the Tigers had raised; the artillery, cannon and aerial firepower; and the Black Tigers' 'life-weapons', their willingness to sacrifice their lives at any given moment, all these put the Movement's confidence at its pinnacle then.

When, following the assassination of Lakshman Kadirgamar, the Western nations including America and Britain proscribed the LTTE, the leadership did not consider it a major problem. When we heard that the Movement had been proscribed, like me, many fighters were upset and confused. The Political Aide Thamilselvan spoke to us in a meeting he had organized, and we were astonished by the message he relayed to us with a laugh: 'Just like you, some of us were deeply troubled and went to meet with anna. Anna laughed and put it to us simply, "We have grown as an international military force to the extent that even these large countries want to ban us; you should think about that and be happy." When we have such a leader, why do we need to be troubled?' The leadership believed we could get past the setback that the vendetta on Kadirgamar had created for the political gains we had made. Everyone was so blinded by their faith in the Tigers' military strength, that they never stopped to consider in the least how it could be possible to attain victory in our struggle for liberation with the whole world as our enemy.

In 2005, Thamilselvan told a meeting of political officers that the Leader had asked us to encourage the people to vote for Mahinda Rajapaksa who was a candidate for President in the upcoming Presidential elections. 'If Mahinda comes to power, there'll definitely be a battle. Instead of being dragged back and forth in talks with these people, if it comes to a fight, we'll win; he's the right man for that.' The words he said then kept coming back to me in the days afterwards.

With Political strategist Anton Balasingham, Adele Balasingham, head of the Transnational Government of Tamil Eelam Rudrakumaran, Political Aide S.P. Thamilselvan, Head of Police P. Nadesan, Head of EROS V. Balakumaran, Judiciary Officer Para, high-ranking Brigadiers Karuna, Thurka, Vithusha and Theepan, Sports Officer Paappa, Political leader Ilamparathi and other key figures

The peace talks that were scheduled for February of 2006 in Geneva were postponed to June. However, as the LTTE was now a proscribed group, it was no longer safe for our delegates to make that journey, and the Movement withdrew from those talks. The talks were postponed further to 28 and 29 October 2006. In the meantime, the government's aerial attacks on Puthukkudiyiruppu and Ananthapuram, and the LTTE's reprisals on the Sinhala population, increased the probability of war.

On 21 July 2006, the gates of the Mavil Aru dam in Trincomalee were closed under the order of Brigadier Sornam of the LTTE. This cut off irrigation to over 15,000 Sinhala farmers' paddy fields. When I was speaking to the political officer for Trincomalee, Ezhilan, about this issue one time, he remarked to me 'Sornam anna said to close the Mavil Aru gates, and the boys did it.' The Mavil Aru incident, which served as an immediate cause for war, had no political or military importance attached to it, but taunted and played with the lives of ordinary Sinhala people.

Brigadier Sornam, who was stationed in Trincomalee, believed that by pulling the Sri Lankan army into war, the Leader would be able to employ the artillery that had been provided to the Trincomalee brigades, launch successful attacks and liberate the areas that were occupied by the army. He had the Leader's approval in this action. As the Movement expected, the final war erupted on the shores of Mavil Arù. On 15 August 2006, the entire Mavil Aru area was captured by the Sri Lankan military, and the war began to expand to the Tiger-controlled areas of Muttur, Sampur, Kattaipparichan and Thoppur. The defeats in Trincomalee were completely the opposite of what the Tigers had anticipated. The Liberation Tigers' excessive confidence in their military prowess received severe blows in Mavil Aru.

On 17 August 2006, Galle Harbour came under ferocious attack from the Sea Tigers. By attacking the harbour with the highest security arrangements, in the completely Sinhala area of Galle, the Sea Tigers hoped to demonstrate the power they held in the ocean surrounding the island of Sri Lanka. The first strikes of the final war were battles in which the Tigers attempted to flex their own strength.

When the A9 was closed in the middle of 2006, the civilians were thrust into a crisis again. The Movement was pushed to the point that they had to win the war at all costs. The peace talks that were scheduled for October 2006 in Geneva were cancelled. War gathered momentum. But the battle that had taken place in Trincomalee had not gone according to the Movement's expectations and was not favourable for the Tigers. As the Sri Lankan army began to capture the Tiger-controlled areas rapidly, the Tigers prepared to face another deadly war. The people were pushed into atrocious conditions again. With no concern for international political or diplomatic conditions at the time, Leader Prabhakaran spoke at the Heroes' Day events in 2006, on the theme 'We will Keep Fighting'. The final war caught on and spread furiously, like a wall of fire.

8

We Lay Down Our Arms

War and fire have the same nature. Once they catch, they see no partiality. They dance their monstrous dance at a velocity of their own. The first phase of the final war between the Liberation Tigers and the Sri Lankan government had reached its end in the eastern province. The army captured all the areas that had been under the control of the Tigers in Trincomalee and Batticaloa. Finally, on 11 July 2007, Kudumbimalai (Thoppigala) also fell to army control. With several hundreds of cadres now dead, Trincomalee Brigadier Sornam, and Batticaloa Brigadier Banu arrived in Vanni with the remaining fighters, carrying the weight of defeat on their backs.

Apart from the Leader of the Tigers, Prabhakaran, and the head of Intelligence, Pottu Amman, the few that still adamantly remained in favour of resuming the war could be counted on one's fingers. Many of the colonels knew too well that the morale of the fighters was very low, even if they didn't show it. The weakened state of the Tigers' attack force did not generate confidence among the colonels and other officers in charge of the frontlines that the war could be won. Brigadier Sornam came under severe criticism among the fighters for having provoked a battle by closing the Mavil Aru dam and then losing so badly to the army.

In the period after 2007, the Vanni plains were the only battleground that remained in the hands of the Tigers. The Movement's store of weapons seemed to have increased, specifically long-range artillery cannons, heavy weaponry and heavy artillery for marine battle. The names for these special weapons were not disclosed to the fighters. Instead, they were referred to by code names like Saarai, Chandiyan, Mongaan and others when they were employed in the battlefields. As we engaged in the final war, it was the weapons and war vessels that carried the confidence of the Movement, rather than the fighters' assault brigades.

After the last days of peace in 2006, the Tigers' artillery ships were being sunk in international waters one after the other. The Sri Lankan Navy kept an eye on the movements of suspicious ships in the Trincomalee harbour area through an ultra-modern radar, in addition to receiving information from the Indian coast guard about the movements of such ships as well. At least three ships carrying arms to the Tigers were destroyed at the edge of international waters by the Sri Lankan Navy. The civilians who heard this complained to us at times, saying 'What is this, children? Our people's money from overseas is being burnt and wasted in the sea like this.' With the Tigers' weapon shipments being repeatedly destroyed, it became impossible to receive the ammunition needed for the artillery cannons and other weapons and use them liberally in the war.

In the first phase of the final war, the artillery and cannons were able to provide support and covering fire for the vanguard attack teams at the battlefront and act as a buttress in their efforts to quash the manoeuvres of the Sri Lankan army. The cannon brigade played a large role in redressing the shortage of manpower among the Tigers, causing heavy losses for the army in the battlefield, and preventing their advancement. In the stages that followed, as a result of the shortage in ammunition, the supporting cover from the rearguard was greatly diminished. For the small number of fighters stationed at defence posts separated by large distances, the volley of artillery fire from the rearguard was a greater boost to their confidence than the guns they held in their own hands. As they saw the advancing army, they immediately called on their divisional command centres to provide shell cover. The middle-tier colonels who were commanding the frontline troops and the artillery brigade ran into serious practical problems. Simultaneously, the vanguard frontline attack troops found themselves unable to withstand the army troops advancing under cover of a rain of shells, wearing bulletproof armour, and volleying fire from PK machine guns which have a very high rate of fire. Consequently, the casualty rate of fighters at the frontlines of the battle were massive. At this juncture, there was no choice for the Tigers' attack forces but to withdraw step by step.

Under the prevailing conditions, Leader Prabhakaran's older son Charles Anthony ramped up efforts to manufacture mortar shells and mines in Ulloor. The Cyber Division, which operated under his leadership, contained the largest number of fighters and greatest financial resources. He was named after a great friend and trusted confidante of the Leader, who had been 2nd Lt. Seelan in the Movement. Charles Anthony's thoughts and practices were very unusual in their approach. He wouldn't worry too much about the practicality or impracticality of a decision. In the final phases of the war, he was considered a hero for his work in forced conscription and on the frontlines, and he was affectionately known as thambi by everyone.

Though the senior colonels had helped raise him from his infancy, Charles Anthony was known to have caused bitter feelings even among them through his affronting behaviour. Brigadier Vithusha disclosed to me several times that in meetings with commanders of the assault brigades, thambi Charles would humiliate the most experienced brigadiers there in the way he expressed his opinions, and she felt uncomfortable witnessing it.

He believed that all civilians should share directly in the work at the frontline. Therefore, he acted on the premise that there need be no hesitations or explanations in the matter of forced conscription. He accused the Political Wing of slacking off, and not working vehemently enough in forced conscription. So, he combined his Cyber Division with the police and undertook forced conscription up to Mullivaikkal. The recruit training bases were also run under his supervision. He went to the frontlines with those fighters. He also attempted to bring in the former fighters who had left or been expelled from the Movement to work with him. Even though it was only for a short period of time, Charles Anthony created a role

During her time of service, Thamizhini with her bodyguards

for himself within the Movement, and functioned within it, with no concern for anything else.

When the Movement decided to practise forced conscription in order to increase its troops in 2006, the civilians saw another terrifying side to them. When the Political Aide announced this at a meeting of the Political Wing, many of the fighters were in shock.

'We have sufficient weapons. We just don't have the troops. If the Leader gets the troops he hopes to get, we will win this war. The Movement has the strength of all three: marine, ground and air forces. We have experienced brigadiers, and above all we have anna. If we only have the troop strength that the Leader expects, this will be the last battle for Tamil Eezham. It isn't enough to have one or two people from each house in the Movement. We need every able-bodied person to pick up a weapon and come forward to do battle. So, you must show no hesitation in enlisting all young men and women into the Movement. It's what the Leader expects.'

When the Political Aide announced the decision to the fighters, I truly could not imagine how the people were going to handle this.

Many other fighters felt the same way. But to express our opinions under those circumstances would have been considered an act of betrayal against the leadership of the Movement. It was believed that the principal duty of a fighter was to put the decisions made by the leadership into practice, rather than create confusion and chaos in the struggle by proffering their own opinions.

Many male and female combatants underwent instructions on how to conduct themselves with civilians while carrying out forced conscription. However, the leadership failed to understand what difficult and terrible work it is to force a young man or woman to join the Movement. There was strong opposition and conflicts between the fighters because of forced conscription. There are no words to describe the conditions of the people who were stuck in Tiger-controlled Vanni during that time. We had taken up arms to protect our society, and we had become the cause of its disintegration.

Marriages between minors were quickly arranged to protect the youth from forced conscription. It even became permissible in our society for young men and women to live together without being married. Parents were forced to set up bunkers and hide their children for months on end to protect them. There were certainly many examples of forcibly conscripted fighters performing extremely valiantly of their own free will. At the same time, there were those who threw down their weapons on the frontlines and ran back home. A few others committed suicide after being forced to go to the frontlines.

To be a fighter in the Political Wing at that time brought me nothing but great anxiety and humiliation. Every single project that the Tigers had done for the good of the people was now completely struck from their memory. I did not believe for a moment that the Movement could gain a victory for the liberation struggle through forced conscription. Instead, I began to dread that we were heading towards an apocalyptic defeat. Because of the Leader's headstrong actions, the people and the fighters were traumatized and confronted with an unbearable wave of losses.

It is my position that forced conscription was the worst of Leader Prabhakaran's poor decisions. Held hostage by circumstances, many fighters and officers kept on reluctantly with the terrible work. Along with the Political Wing, the Assault Brigade leaders were also furiously engaged in conscription. When I attempted to share the civilians' concerns with a senior colonel at a meeting in Puthukkudiyiruppu, he said to me: 'Thamizhini, why are you so confused? We are doing what the Leader asks of us. If you are unable to do the task, please leave it and go, don't confuse others as well.'

After more bitter experiences and the mental strain that followed, I found myself unable to work with the same degree of enthusiasm as before. Political Aide Thamilselvan said to me: 'Thamizhini, you should pay more attention to the work related to women. We can have another officer take care of this work.' The news gave me a great sense of peace. I felt a constriction in my chest loosen up, and my mind and body felt more at ease. Rather than continue as an officer and become emotionally affected by organizational problems, I felt it would be more appropriate to be a fighter and do work happily for women. A senior fighter from the assault brigade was made head of the Women's Political Wing.

I thought I must put my freedom to good use. I spent many days with the Women's Brigade that stood at the frontline. I participated in the Movement's propaganda meetings and in the important meetings of the Political Wing. I had come to understand, from my experiences as a head of the Women's Political Wing, that it was impossible to consider the entire dimensions of our struggle and act accordingly when caught in the pressures of demanding organizational work, and instead we exhausted ourselves in the work assigned to us. As the Liberation Tigers' Movement lost its character as a revolutionary organization, and transformed itself into a political machine, a lot of the Movement's intellectual power was wasted, entangled in bureaucratic knots. Many brilliant fighters were given appointments as officers and wasted their time and skill dealing with organizational hiccups. But that was considered the growth and the pride of the Movement. During times of peace, I know that many who came from abroad were thrilled that they saw another nation north of Omanthai.

From the time I joined the Movement, Brigadier Vithusha treated me as a friend with whom she could speak openly. Though she was a senior in the Movement, and more experienced, she was a sympathetic colonel to many female officers like me. Her birthplace was the village of Kappoothu in Vadamaradchi. The eldest daughter of a prominent Hindu Brahmin family, she told us that she joined the Movement after being deeply affected by the Kumuthini boat massacre. While she began her early activities as part of the 'Freedom Birds', she received her combat training in the second training base of the Liberation Tigers, near Kilali. She was a perfectionist with any work she was assigned.

During the time when the Indian military was in Sri Lanka, when the Liberation Tigers' Movement was hidden in the Manal Aru forest, she was responsible for the storehouses. After that, from the attack on Jaffna fort, until 2009 when she lost her life in Ananthapuram in Puthukkudiyiruppu, she played a prominent role in every assault the Women's Brigade was engaged in. Though, in the beginning, she was only in charge of smaller assault teams in the Women's Brigade, she grew step by step to become one of the chief commanding brigadiers of the Movement. She was a Second Level Colonel in the Women's Brigade in 1993 and became Special Brigadier of the Malathi Brigade and served to the end. Her own brother Vithushan died a Hero's death in a battle with the army in Vilakkuvaithakulam in Vavuniya in 1999.

Though I did not have many opportunities to participate in frontal assault actions, I would occasionally go to Brigadier Vithusha's command centre when she was operating on the battlefield and discuss the hostilities with her. In the final stages of the war, I was able to sense that Brigadier Vithusha was experiencing a lot of internal turmoil. During 2007, her Malathi Brigade was stationed at the frontlines in Mannar. Every time I had to visit the political cadres based in Mannar district, I would stop by her command centre. She had the opportunity to speak to the Leader directly about the field conditions and about the activities of the Malathi Brigade. She complained to me: 'No one informs the Leader about the full extent of the hostilities at the frontlines, or the administrative difficulties.' Brigadier Vithusha had a practice of keeping the Leader fully informed on the facts, the problems encountered in the frontlines and the crises faced by the fighters.

When the Leader queried the male brigadiers on these problems, it tended to be embarrassing for many of the senior brigadiers. Under the guise of offering advice, they would make digs at her: 'It's up to us to address the issues on the frontlines. Vithusha takes all the problems to anna. He's overburdened with problems already; we shouldn't add to his tension.' These kinds of incidents caused Vithusha a lot of stress.

Vithusha, who had begun her life as an armed combatant at the age of 18, was close to 40 at the beginning of the last stages of the war. Having borne the scars from many battles on her body, the life of repeated, prolonged crises in the battlefields, the daily encounters with losses and the ceaseless war created an internal fatigue in her that was shared by many long-time cadres. Sometimes Vithusha would turn to me and voice her extreme frustration. Once, when we were talking at her command centre in the Andakulam area of Mannar, she turned to me and said, 'Do you think we'll win this fight?' I kept looking at her for a while. 'Why, girl, did we end up with this kind of life? The world has moved somewhere, and here we are dying in the jungles and the mud.' This brave woman Brigadier, with her questions for which there were no easy answers, took part in the Liberation Tigers final long-range penetration attack and died a Hero's death; her corpse lay unattended for defeat to peck away at and devour.

Many of the senior male Brigadiers who were approaching 50 were also heading towards a state of despair. The high pressure of the battlefield, their irregular dietary habits and constant movement had left them with permanent health problems like high blood pressure, kidney disease and spinal injuries. Brigadier Balraj, the vanguard marshal who had led many successful attacks for the Liberation Tigers became critically ill with kidney disease and other complications and died unexpectedly in 2008. It would not be untruthful to say that an increase in second-level colonels was completely lacking. While many skilful male and female combatants advanced in the ranks to higher commands, it was much more common for them to lose their lives in a very short time on the battlefields.

Many administrative units and newer and newer assault squads were formed in the Movement in keeping with the Leader's wishes. But there was insufficient cadre strength for what was needed. A certain number of colonels and cadres took the bulk of the work on their own shoulders. As a result, we were unable to keep up with the necessary training or additional preparations, and the overall efficiency of the Movement diminished. Despite the current reality, the image of the Tigers as an impressive military force prevailed, based on their past victories. The confidence of the diasporic people was unwavering on this issue. While the image of the Tigers' military strength was spread to the outside world through modern electronic media, creating a sense of awe to the outside gaze, the reality was that it had turned to grass inside.

In 2007, Political Aide Thamilselvan and seven fighters working with him died in an aerial bombing attack by the Sri Lankan Air Force. The loss of Thamilselvan was devastating to the Leader. He was a fighter of unflinching loyalty, who carried out the Leader's every tenet without any questions. He supervised and carried out many of the Leader's specific tasks himself. I had worked in his charge in the administration of the Political Wing from 1993. I was as affected by his death as I would have been by the death of my own brother. Whenever he explained a project to us, he would refer to the Leader word for word, saying: 'Anna expects this. We must act accordingly.' A highly skilled marksman, he received his training in India and was part of the Leader's team of bodyguards. In 1993, the Political Wing that had been under Mahattaya was handed over to him. He remained the Political Aide for the Liberation Tigers' Movement until his final days.

I know that he followed the Leader's beliefs to the letter in his attitude towards the female cadres. Thamilselvan raised me from a highly inexperienced fighter to the level of an officer. He had the ability to figure out a person's skills, encourage them, and give them the opportunities to develop them even further. When he gave out a task, he didn't waste time distinguishing between men and women. In many critical projects he assigned female fighters as equals of male fighters.

In 1994, I was operating in the Education Division in the Lingam base in Kokuvil. Suddenly I was told that Aide Thamilselvan was asking for me. I knew some higher-up officers had come there to meet him. I was an ordinary fighter. I ran fearfully, wondering why he was calling me. 'Come here, thangachi. I'm going to give you some important work; I have appointed you for some propaganda work in the Point Pedro District. You must take charge and do what's needed. I will give you all the help you need. You must start work right away.' He explained the work I had to do and sent me off. The way the project was structured, to have men and women working together, gave me new and enlightening experiences.

After I was appointed head of the Women's Political Wing, he did not patronize me as someone he had mentored but treated me with the respect appropriate to my responsibilities. As a result, I was able to hold my head up and advance even among the male divisional heads. When I ran into conflicts over projects with other officers, he would always give his opinions from a neutral stance. After his sudden death, the head of the police force, Mr. Nadesan was appointed Political Aide. He too was someone deeply trusted by the Leader.

In September 2007, the military manoeuvres undertaken by the Sri Lankan army, beginning in Mannar, advanced rapidly and violently through great stretches of land. Unlike before, the army employed cunning deep-penetration attacks, and quickly began to capture areas that had been under our control. The intricacies of the Vanni forests that had been an advantage for the Tigers in the time of the army's 'Jayasikuru' operation were now well known and understood by the army. While on the one hand, the military was continuously engaged in advance manoeuvres to capture the areas that had been under Tiger control, on the other hand, they were attempting to destroy the Tigers rearguard with several claymore attacks and aerial attacks.

The army's long-range reconnaissance patrol targeted and carried out claymore attacks on the roads used for travel by the Tigers' frontline colonels, officers, and the fighters' aid teams, as well as for transporting heavy weaponry. The army's claymore attacks were also severe on the transport routes behind the vanguard checkpoints. Sometimes the claymore attacks were followed by heavy weapon attacks on the same target. Brigadier Balraj miraculously escaped such an attack on the A9 road.

The first claymore attack I personally witnessed was on the road from Puthukkudiyiruppu to Oddusuddan. Another female fighter and I were travelling by an MD90 motorbike to a female fighters' base in Oddusuddan. Our kerosene-filled bike rose and fell like a boat in the sea because the road was full of bumps and hollows and covered in gravel. It was past eight in the morning. There were no pedestrians at all on the road. The two of us were talking loudly over the sound of the motorbike engine as we went. I was seated in the back and was thrown onto the road by the force of a great explosion behind us. We thought there must have been some terrible accident behind us and turned our bike around and went in that direction. There, the Leader's bodyguard was frantically involved in a hurried search operation. They stopped us from going any further. Our hearts were pounding. It was an area close to the small side street where the Leader's base was set up. When we asked a fighter whom we knew what had happened, he told us to go see for ourselves.

A vehicle hit by a claymore stood with its front completely smashed in. A slightly stocky, lifeless body was propped up against the side of the vehicle. The face was caved in and the jaw hung open. When we saw his build and the frame of the vehicle, we realized who it was, and stood stunned in an unbearable state of shock. Colonel Shankarappa, the special colonel of the Liberation Tigers' Air Wing, lost his life in that attack. An aeronautical engineer, he had come from London to join the Movement. His younger brother Haran was one of the 12 Tigers, including Colonels Kumarappa and Pulenthiran, who had taken cyanide and committed suicide in 1987.

It was through Colonel Sankar's hard work that the Tigers Air Wing was founded. The Ampakamam forest area was completely under his control. He had also constructed an airport in that forest area, near Iranamadu. He was the person who had taught the first fighters how to move through a dense forest with the help of a compass, and how to safeguard top secrets. Unlike other colonels, he could speak freely with the Leader. He was also a trusted advisor to many colonels and captains. He would speak to me very affectionately. He had often praised me after hearing my speeches on stage; he advised me to read many books. He gave us books to read like *Leningrad, Stalingrad*, and ask questions of the fighters whenever he spotted us; many cadres would quietly slip away whenever they saw him. His death was a tremendous loss to the Movement and to the struggle.

The Tigers came to realize that the army's long-range reconnaissance patrol had acquired very detailed and precise information about the Tigers' most important locations. The covert attack operations carried out in such a strategic manner in the high-security zone of Puthukkudiyiruppu, which was many kilometres away from the frontlines of the battlefield, and the claymore mines discovered in several important locations confirmed the Tigers' suspicions.

While the battle was proceeding in Mannar, the Tigers found evidence of the long-range reconnaissance patrol in the Vallipunam forest area of Puthukkudiyiruppu as well. In those circumstances, the news stunned the inner circle of the LTTE. The Tigers understood that the Leader himself was marked as the main target of the final war. As a result, unlike in peace times, when the Leader carried out his meetings somewhat openly, while the final war continued, these were completely reinedin, and meetings were limited only to the high-ranking colonels. At the same time, his bodyguard and troops were strengthened.

It became necessary, because of these threatening moves by the long-range reconnaissance patrol, to be extra vigilant in fortifying the internal security of the areas under Movement control. As the Movement was severely short of cadres, civilians were largely used for internal security. The Tigers' internal intelligence tasks were escalated as well. Street surveillance teams were stationed at night and people were searched as well. The Tigers' special teams set up secret posts in the densest areas of the forest and took up surveillance operations. Occasionally there were skirmishes when they encountered evidence of the Long Range Reconnaissance Patrol (LRRP). However, the Tigers were not able to stop the LRRP's advancement.

For up to 50 metres on either side of the main roads in Vanni, including the A9 highway, the forests were cut down, the ground levelled, and the auxiliary troop defence posts were set up along the length of the road. From Murikandy to Iranamadu, the women of the auxiliary forces had set up defence posts as well. The cadres were put in charge of this operation. A colonel who was familiar with the terrain of the Vanni forests was put in charge of internal security operations. However, the LRRPs avoided the predicted routes and tampered with other critical areas, creating shockwaves among the Tigers. Until the last stage of the war, the Tigers were not able to halt the operations of the LRRPs.

In the same way, many of the Tigers' operations were sabotaged by the Sri Lankan Air Force attacks. The spy planes (drones) would begin flying overhead from dawn. The small aircraft which were impossible to spot, and operated by remote control, was usually called 'bug' by the cadres. The Sri Lankan Air Force took aim at the colonels' main bases, the training grounds of the attack teams, the basic training camps and the rearguard's administrative centres and launched precision attacks on them. The Movement was stunned when even the secret bases in the densest forest areas, despite the height of camouflage, were struck.

One time, as another cadre and I were travelling by motorbike along Vallipunam road, we were thrown off our bike by the blasts of the bombs being dropped by the airplanes that appeared screeching loudly overhead. The Liberation Tigers' headquarters, which had been highly camouflaged in the small forest area by the side of the Vallipunam road had been blown to pieces. It was the Liberation Tigers' main administrative centre, where all the administrative work done by the leadership was brought together by the head secretariat.

I have memories of being caught up in more air strikes and claymore attacks than I can number. But it was pure luck, and nothing else, that prevented me from getting injured or killed. Sometimes the clothes I was wearing would be torn, or even the motorbike I was on, was damaged. I have also had many days where I was made completely deaf. I had a permanent internal injury on my left knee from when I had fallen and hurt it. Another time I was unconscious for a whole day because of a blow to the back of my head. My friends teased me that I had rambled nonsense during that time. The machine gun bullets and shrapnel that were meant for me missed me by a hair's breadth. I have picked them up in my hands and felt their heat. In times of great distress and exhaustion I wondered why it was that this difficult life kept stretching on as some sort of bonus.

In the latter part of 2007, I was given an invitation to a meeting with Political Aide Nadesan. It was given out that the meeting would take place in the Peace Secretariat in Paravippanchan in Kilinochchi. A few minutes before the appointed time, I arrived there alone on my motorcycle. The whole compound was deserted. As I wondered what to do, there was a roar like a tsunami wave coming down from the sky. As soon as I realized there was going to be an air strike, even if I wanted to get out of there in a hurry, I didn't have enough time to get my motorcycle going. Since the street was obviously full of Movement camps, I didn't think that running out would be a good idea either. I thought somehow that day was going to be the day I died. When the aircraft swooped to drop bombs, I flattened myself on the ground under a small tree. I prayed: 'God, don't let me be injured and lose my limbs, let me die quickly.' A section of the Peace Secretariat building shrank and collapsed as though it had rotted. Pieces of glass and rocks shattered and flew. A circle of smoke reeking of sulphur covered that place. I opened my eyes slowly and brushed myself off. I shook my hands and legs to check if I had any injuries: nothing. My motorcycle had just a few dents as well. I later heard that the meeting had been moved to a different location at the last minute, and that I had accidentally been sent word too late.

The bases critical to the Movement had undergone air strikes more than once. The Sea Tigers' base was so severely under attack that we could not go near it. The administrative office of the Malathi Brigade, which was situated near Visuvamadu, was reduced to rubble in an airstrike. A house in that area, that had initially been set aside with high security arrangements for the Leader's meetings, was given over for the Malathi Brigade's administrative office shortly after. There, Brigadier Vithusha called me and a few other officers for a hurried meeting before she left. The next day that house too was struck with precision.

As part of our civilian self-defence training and aiding a civilian force in reconstruction, we conducted training for students as well. Once, when the training in self-defence and first aid was being carried out for more than a hundred female students from the areas of Puthukkudiyiruppu, Vallipunam and Sencholai, the building was bombed by the air force. More than 50 schoolgirls, advanced-level students, died in that attack. Many escaped with serious injuries. The catastrophe that resulted from the hurried actions of the Movement to train auxiliary forces without thinking through the security of these students sufficiently, or without proper planning, was devastating. The loss felt by their parents, who cuddled those children on their laps and raised them with so many dreams, was the height of anguish that tore away at our hearts.

Due to the shortage of cadres at the frontlines, there were long gaps between the Movement's vanguard security posts. As some sections were considered less dangerous, the fighters did rounds in those areas rather than be stationed at a security post. As a result, the army was able to carry out covert manoeuvres in some places and capture the area. While the battle continued in the Mannar district, some special attacks and Black Tiger attacks were carried out simultaneously.

Many assaults were launched at the time, including the Anuradhapura airport attack, and the artillery attack on the Vavuniya military base. It was believed that these special attacks would shatter the rearguard of the military operations just as they had done in the past. But the army quickly recovered and began preparing itself for the next phase of attack. The Tigers had taken on heightened preparations for the Anuradhapura airport attack and employed highly effective Black Tigers. The air force suffered losses, as the Movement had anticipated. However, within the following week, the Sri Lankan government had acquired a new class of aircraft and increased the strength of its air force. In the last phase of the war, every plan of the Movement seemed to have the inverse effect from what had been anticipated.

By that time, due to the onslaught of the military's aerial and ground attacks the Movement found itself in a situation where it was unable to combine its troops to strategize a powerful counter strike. Though some training plans were undertaken on the sea and land to carry out such a special operation, it became necessary to hurriedly employ those troops in the continuing attacks on the vanguard security posts.

In 2008, the Black Tigers planned an operation to strike hard at the Colombo harbour. The intelligence had been surveyed and the Black Tiger cadre were sent out. However, that attack did not turn out as the Movement hoped. As the Black Tigers did not get the targets they needed to attack, they had to return to Vanni. This led to an incident where those Black Tigers were detained by Admiral Soosai and put through rigorous interrogation as well. Female Black Tigers were included in this as well. In the last days of the war, following peace times, the Movement met with these kinds of debacles as well.

A massive sand barrier was set up in the Mulankavil area and attacks were planned with the intent of halting the advancing army. Following that, similar sand barriers were set up in the Akkarayan and Vanneri areas as well. Civilians who had been enlisted in these areas were given this work as compulsory duties. The military attacks aimed at those areas led to many losses, serious injuries and loss of limbs. In those circumstances where their families had to move, there was a tendency for male householders to not come forward for border patrol or other frontline activities. Though the Movement offered higher payment to the border patrollers, they still hesitated to go to the frontlines. For this reason, the Movement began coercively engaging them in forced labour. By October 2008, the Akkarayan area was captured by the military.

The displacements, the poverty, being stuck in war, and fearing for their lives, all took a heavy toll on the civilians. In the last days of the war, the Movement did not think or act in a way that considered the civilians at all. The political cadres were only used to drag everyone in sight to the battlegrounds at that stage.

On 23 November 2008, the military began attacks on Kilinochchi. On 2 January 2009, Kilinochchi town and the areas adjoining it had completely fallen to the military. Many among the colonels, cadres and civilians believed that the Leader had a plan to allow the army to sneak well into the Tigers' area and then launch an assault. Even among the Tamils in the diaspora, such an expectation was widespread: 'They're going to let them in and strike for sure.' However, when Eezhappiriyan, who had been part of Political Aide Thamilselvan's team of bodyguards, and after his death grew into a highly skilled assault fighter, met me for the last time in Kilinochchi, he shared something the Leader had disclosed to him: 'Everyone thinks everything is in my hands. I have nothing. My hands are empty,' the Leader had said, opening out his hands. Eezhappiriyan opened out his own hands as he told me this story. 'If anna himself says this, what can we do?' he said sorrowfully as he left. A few days later, that young fighter Eezhappiriyan, with the valour of Abhimanyu of the Mahabharata, fought off the army that surrounded him and attained a Hero's death. We have no choice but to admit that there was no military manoeuvre the Tigers could have undertaken to sustain Kilinochchi. The massive water tank that had been constructed in the centre of the town during peace times had been smashed by a bomb placed by the Movement. During the advance operations of the Sath Jaya troops, the Tigers had bombed the previous tank that had existed there. In 2008, Kilinochchi was annihilated again. The civilians were uprooted and moved to Tharmapuram, which was 13 kilometers from Kilinochchi.

At the insistence of Political Aide Nadesan, and under order of the Leader, I resumed my service as head of the Women's Political Wing in January of 2008. With the sudden loss of Political Aide Thamilselvan following the death of political strategist Anton Balasingham from cancer in 2007, any close and direct communications the Tigers' Movement had with peace brokers in the Western world was completely severed.

Nadesan, who had been appointed Political Aide after Thamilselvan's death, maintained close connections with the forces supporting Tamil Eezham in Tamil Nadu. He was very confident that his political activities would save the Movement from this state of crisis. The Tiger leadership had been convinced that when Jayalalitha became Chief Minister of Tamil Nadu in the elections that were due to happen in 2009, she would put pressure on the central government and bring about an immediate ceasefire between the Sri Lankan government and the Tigers. Nadesan had that much faith in the words of Tamil Nadu politicians. However, I had no faith that the sympathetic powers in Tamil Nadu could bring about that kind of immediate change. It could not be expected that their emotional speeches and the immolating sacrifices of allies like Muthukumar and Senkody would shift the attention of the Indian government.

Having forgotten that in Tamil Nadu, popular political leaders ingratiate themselves with allies of Tamil Eezham simply to use them to fill up their ballot boxes in election times, our leader Prabhakaran was left abandoned, despairing whether even a straw could be grasped in the waves of this sea. After Poonakari was captured by the Sri Lankan army in November of 2008, the troops advanced toward Paranthan, capturing all the land routes to Jaffna, including Elephant Pass on 31 December, and thereby the entire province. From there they began advancing toward Kilinochchi. On 2 January 2009, Kilinochchi, which had been the peace time capital of the Tigers, fell completely to the army. The President of Sri Lanka, Mahinda Rajapaksa gave the Liberation Tigers an ultimatum to lay down their arms and surrender.

Following this, the army captured Tharmapuram without any great struggle. The civilians sought refuge in the Suthanthirapuram, Udayarkattu and Vallipunam areas. At this time, the Tigers' plan to explode the Visuvamadu dam using the Black Tigers, and submerge the army that was breaking through, also met with defeat. The Tigers' Voice gave out misinformation that hundreds of army personnel had lost their lives, with the hope of generating some confidence in the people. The civilians were in a state of anxiety not knowing which direction they could move in, and with what expectations. The Tigers were rendered helpless and could no longer give any kind of firm assurance to the people.

As the Movement was unable to find any other places to set up their artillery and cannon to open shellfire on the army, they based them in places like Suthanthirapuram, Vallipunam and

Devipuram. As the army returned their artillery strikes with shell attacks and aerial attacks, the civilians crowded for refuge in those areas were killed in large numbers. The blood of the very people we went to fight for, overflowed like rivers upon the soil. We could not comfort ourselves with any kind of justification for the war we were engaged in now.

At that moment I came to hate the armed struggle. We were at a point where the whole race could be wiped out because of the decisions taken by the leadership. Civilians had been killed during the 30 years; they had been slaughtered by the hundreds of thousands. They had lost millions in property, many hundreds of thousands of people had seen their futures be annihilated. These were all sacrifices the people had made for freedom. But, after our people were destroyed, for whom was this nation? For whom was this freedom? I could not accept the calamities our people were undergoing in the last days of the war. I saw before my very eyes that the form of our struggle was wrong. Our beloved people lay as abandoned corpses by the roadsides, before our eyes. Our armed struggle was one of the reasons for it. But then, for whom was this struggle?

The veteran fighters had reached the pinnacle of hate. Many of the new fighters who had been forcibly recruited and had undergone insufficient training were unable to withstand the frontlines, and a large number left their weapons and returned home. The civilian shelters, which had already shrunk quite a lot, had now turned into battlegrounds wherever you looked. From moment to moment you heard the wails of loss. The Movement was heading towards its demise in a very pathetic state.

One after another, events piled up that truly crushed and ground down the dream that the armed struggle would bring us freedom. The civilians who had moved about as they were instructed to by the Tigers now felt utterly disgusted by them. There was no room to stretch out your legs, not a handful of food to satisfy the hunger in your belly, no guarantee of survival even for a moment; under these conditions, the people began to move towards the military-controlled areas. At first, they began to move out in large numbers through the Iruttumadu area in the Udayarkattu district.

We were immediately instructed by the leadership to put a halt to their departure. The political cadres were rushed out for this. Nobody understood what sort of words of confidence we could utter to convince the people to stop leaving. Were we to keep the people in jeopardy in order to fight for the people? If so, for whose safety was this war being fought? The answer to that question rose up as a terrifying apparition before me. A male captain secretly said to me: 'Thamizhini akka, the people are knocking us down and leaving, if we try to physically stop them, they'll beat us down and keep going. I thought to myself, let the people who are leaving go and survive, and I stayed quiet.' Many other cadres, like myself, shared that fighter's feelings. Yet, I said nothing to him, and remained silent.

The army began to advance towards Suthanthirapuram. The Movement informed the people in that area not to go towards the military-held area, but to move through the Iranaipalai areas instead. The civilians, who suffered from injuries and deaths because of the attacks that continued throughout the day, kept moving. Many of the Tiger bases were set up in Suthanthirapuram. The attack squads were based in the Suthanthirapuram school area.

Three of us female cadres and two male cadres were staying in the civilian shelter area. Most of the civilians had left the area by then. Here and there a few families were getting ready for the journey. In the night's gentle moonlight, we could see people winding their way through the paddy fields. One of the Tiger's ammunition stores in the Udayarkattu area exploded into smithereens and the ensuing flames rose high into the sky as it burned. Unusually, there was no sound of fire at all at that time. The quiet was terrifying in those circumstances. The fighters stood along the Suthanthirapuram school fence, prepared for a battle that could break out at any minute. Brigadier Vithusha stood there with the fighters of the Malathi Brigade. We went across to meet her and exchange some messages.

Vithusha akka, who had been in great emotional turmoil burst into tears when she saw me. 'I'm ashamed to think what the Movement has come to. I don't have any answers for the questions these girls ask me,' she said in a furiously bitter tone I had never heard from her before. 'The people are going to the army, unable to bear any more, and the Movement is telling us to shoot below their feet if they're going. My god, with what mind can I tell someone to shoot at the people. Even then, when I gave them the news that the Movement tells us to do this, the girls say "Why akka, are we to shoot our mothers, fathers and siblings? It's better if we shoot ourselves and die first," and they're in a mess. It's true, girl. The Movement has been reduced to such a shameful state,' she wailed. The image of her, heartbroken as she was that day, remains in my mind's eye. Exhausted in body and mind I turned back after speaking with her.

I got a walkie talkie from Vithusha akka and gave it to one of the male cadres who had come with me. We had to cross an expansive paddy field and return to Suthanthirapuram road. The situation was still calm. It made me suspicious that there may be armed forces hidden somewhere around. I thought it best if we split up into two teams to travel. As we walked through the paddy fields, I kept contact with the male cadres through a walkie talkie. A bullet came whistling out of nowhere and hit the levee right beside where I was seated. I realized that the army was very close to us. It dawned on me that the army had secretly advanced behind us, without the strike teams on the vanguard realizing it. Under these circumstances I couldn't resume contact with the male cadres who had come with us. Because I couldn't talk on the walkie, I tried calling out in a slightly raised voice, 'Thambi…'. We began moving in the direction they had set off in, with the hope that we'd find them somehow.

After we had gone some distance, we observed two shadowy figures standing very still. Thinking that they might be the male cadres who had come with us, I began moving towards the shadowy figures. 'Akka…don't go that way,' one of the cadres I had gone in search of shouted out, stopped, grabbed me and hurriedly pulled me backwards. After we had run some short distance away, we regrouped. 'Akka, it's the army over there. The people are going over to the army, it seems. That's why they're so quiet. We went up close and came running back to tell you,' he said. After that, I informed Vithusha akka of the situation and hurried back to move the injured cadres who were in my care. When dawn broke, all Suthanthirapuram had been captured by the army. The Movement had hoped to engage in a battle and stop the army's advancement, and we had been unable to do so.

In the Iranaipalai and Ananthapuram areas of Puthukkudiyiruppu district, the civilians were in overcrowded quarters with barely any space between them. In the Vallipunam area, because of the shelling directed at the Mullaitivu main road that travelled through Puthukkudiyiruppu, the Landmasters and tractors belonging to the displaced civilians were ruined. Pots and pans and other household items lay scattered with civilian corpses and animal carcasses all along the roads. A terrible stench permeated the whole district. The people travelling from Suthanthirapuram to Iranaipalai moved through the forest pathways of Devipuram. Since there were some important Sea Tiger bases and artillery stations in that area, the Sri Lankan air force kept up an endless aerial attack. During one of those attacks, the cadre travelling with me, and I, escaped by a hair's breadth with our lives.

I saw Brigadier Vithusha again at a medical camp based in Iranaipalai. She said she had returned from seeing the Leader after a long time. I wondered where the Leader was, during this crisis. But I didn't ask. The cadres never had the habit of asking for the whereabouts of the Leader.

The Leader had told her, 'We'd need 25,000 trained combatants and artillery shells to recapture Kilinochchi,' said Vithusha in a voice devoid of any expression. 'Listening to the stories Pottu Amman tells will drive you crazy. I have lost any shred of respect I had for him. He keeps talking without any sense of reality.'

She went silent, not knowing what else she could say. It was clear to see that the agonies suffered by the civilians had affected her terribly. Her eyes, fiery red with the loss of sleep, were brimming with tears as she sighed, 'The poor people.' It is very hard to describe that moment of frustration. That was our last meeting.

'   In the last days of the war, it was obvious that the other brigadiers were furious with chief of intelligence, Pottu Amman. The orders he gave, with no sense of the vulnerabilities of the troops generated

Thamizhini with Brigadier Thurka and other fighters at a rally held by the Tigers

a lot of anger. He put forward the idea that the cadres who had lost their limbs should set up stations around Puthukkudiyiruppu. He ordered that they blow themselves up when the army advanced. He had also told the Black Tigers to take claymore explosives to the vanguard to launch attacks at the army. In this way many fighters went to the frontline posts and meaninglessly lost their lives in a war that couldn't be won. The Leader had once said: 'I have created the Black Tigers as the powerful weapon of a weakened people.' One Black Tiger hero had driven a vehicle filled with explosives into the military checkpoint on Keppapilavu road in Puthukkudiyiruppu and blown himself up with the intention of destroying the checkpoint. None of these kinds of attacks had the effect of stopping the advancement of the military, and because Pottu Amman wouldn't acknowledge the realities of the battlefield, these actions led to the meaningless sacrifice of fighters' lives.

When peace was disrupted and war loomed over us again, the movie *300*, which had been dubbed by the Tigers' film translation division, was screened at a gathering with the Leader. At the same time, movies like *Hitler's Last Days* were also dubbed and shown to the fighters. The world watched in disbelief at the way the Liberation Tigers of Tamil Eelam, the splendid movement for freedom, became paralysed. I have even wondered if the Leader dreamt of defeat while he began the final war. The blood and tears of hundreds of thousands of people had watered the Movement's growth. That being so, what a terrible catastrophe had been brought about by keeping the Liberation Tigers' Movement and the armed struggle for the Tamil people at the mercy of the likes and dislikes of a single man, and guided by his decisions alone?

Around the third month of 2009, Pottu Amman conducted a meeting for all the officers at a camp based in Puthukkudiyiruppu. Puthukkudiyiruppu, which had been the highest security zone of the Liberation Tigers Movement, had now turned into a high-risk battleground. The meeting did not take long that day. Pottu Amman put forward the following points in a very concise manner: 'Unless some miracle happens, it is not realistic anymore that the Movement will win; those of you who have documents related to the Movement, destroy them completely; the people have begun going over to the army. When the time comes for the Tigers to go across with them, they will ask "If there's a Tiger here, get up"; when you get up and tell them "I'm a Tiger", they will shoot you; that's what will happen. The leadership is making every effort to turn the battle around. However, I repeat, understand one thing very clearly; it is unlikely that we will win unless some miracle happens. I'm not saying this to upset you. I'm telling you the truth of the situation; most importantly, I have called you here today to tell you to destroy the documents that are with you.'

With that the meeting ended. There was not a word said about the injured fighters or those who had remained in the care homes trusting in the Movement. The double danger facing the female cadres was not spoken about either. We disbanded and left in such a state it didn't occur to us to even speak to each other. That was the last meeting of the heads of the Liberation Tigers in Puthukkudiyiruppu.

After the Puthukkudiyiruppu district was captured by the army, the Tigers undertook a penetrative attack in the Ananthapuram area. Brigadier Banu led the operation, in which many of the top-ranking brigadiers participated on the ground. In the attack, which lasted three days, many fighters died, including many senior brigadiers. Only brigadier Banu and a few fighters escaped with their lives. Colonels Vithusha, Thurka, Manivannan, Gadaffi and many other fighters lost their lives in the attack. Their bodies could not be retrieved, and they were abandoned there. Special Brigadier of the artillery troops Pavanithi, Kittu, who had participated in the attack, told me that they were forced to abandon several injured fighters as well.

After Kilinochchi was lost the civilian dwelling areas became the frontlines of the war. All the Movement's activities were carried out right in the middle of the civilian crowds. Forced conscription was underway with a vengeance as far away as Mullivaikkal. Basic training was undertaken in the palmyrah groves in that area. The training had come down to the level that it sufficed to be able to hold a weapon in your hands and pull a trigger. Though we knew that these actions were utterly useless and would only lead to more unnecessary casualties, these actions were undertaken with a tenacious determination. As a result, the fighters and the civilians felt complete despair. Many experienced fighters began to quit the Movement. Those who had gone to join their families and mixed in with the civilian population were informed that if they did not return to their activities within the Movement, they would face execution. Some such incidents happened among the Sea Tigers.

The Tigers' Voice radio was announcing the uplifting news that a ship, the Vanangaman, organized by the diasporic community, was to arrive with relief supplies for the people. In that moment of crisis, the Tigers' Voice radio played many programmes and relayed news that would give the people some courage. The people complained and caused a stampede hoping to somehow get permission to go aboard the ship that had been organized by the Red Cross to carry away the sick and injured. Many fighter families were engaged in efforts to at least get their children sent off safely. People kept moving out by sea and land without the Movement's knowledge. No matter how hard the Movement tried to stop them, or threaten them with gunfire, the people went so far as to pull their children out of the Movement and leave with them.

My mother had developed a growth in her uterus and had undergone a hysterectomy, but within six months of the surgery she was displaced from our house, which was in Kanakapuram in Kilinochchi. She moved about from place to place, and finally some cadres I knew told me that they had seen her, carrying a small bag, standing all alone on Vadduvakal beach. When my mother had seen me once in the Puthumathalan area, she had begun sobbing, saying to me: 'Let's go the way the people are going, child, I don't have anyone left but you.' We didn't know the whereabouts of my brothers' or sisters' families; we had no idea what might have happened to them. When I saw my mother in Mullivaikkal, she showed me her feet, scratched and gashed by thorns. She said that these injuries had happened as she and some others ran along the forest paths in Devipuram. She had a cloth over her head to shield herself from the sun and was standing in line with an aluminium pan to receive some porridge. My mind was tortured by the thought that we had gone to fight for the nation and become responsible for the helpless state of the mothers who had borne us.

Civilians broke into the Movement's stores and began taking out the things they needed. People who had treated us with respect and affection because we were fighters had now got to such a point of anger and hatred that they began to turn on the Liberation Tigers with open hostility: 'Yes, we're going to the army. What are you going to do about it? We came so far trusting in you. Now where are you telling us to go; what is your leader going to do?'

The people's desperation came out as angry words and overflowed in tears. There were occasions where they grabbed hold of their children who were in the Movement, and dragged them away by force in their rage, saying: 'You've done enough with your fighting, come now!' Even though the Movement could not accomplish anything at this point, they kept carrying out their efforts to stop civilians from evacuating the area. The people were trapped in such a crowded mass that if one shell fell and exploded, over 10 people could be killed.

On the 9 May 2009, at around seven at night, Political Aide Nadesan called a few officers for an urgent meeting under a small tree in a sandy area on the shores of Mullivaikkal, where his bunker was situated. The moon shone as bright as day. The people had created some shelters nearby by tightly tying up some plastic mats together. We had been advised that the fighters should gather in small groups here and there between those shelters and keep watch. The Tigers believed that instead of launching larger attacks on the army, they could engage in covert penetration to recapture the areas where the people were crowded together.

As the meeting was going on, a bright light turned the night into day. Some shells had hit the area where the Tigers' fuel barrels had been buried, and exploded, and the area was ablaze like a bonfire. Some weapons that had been close by also exploded as they caught fire. The ferocity of the flames stretched over us where we stood as well. We scattered. I heard something buzzing like an insect over my head; I turned my head to look. A piece of shrapnel fell plop to the ground just in front of me. If I had not turned my head a fraction, that speeding piece of shrapnel would have caught me square in the head. I picked it up and looked at it. It was boiling hot like a live piece of coal.

I met the Political Aide in Mullivaikkal for the last time on 13 May 2009. For a few days, there had been no reassuring words from him about any help from India. He was quiet for a long time. When I looked at his face, I could tell that he was struggling because he was unable to tell us some serious news. As we waited, there were some attacks nearby and he asked us to disband quickly and sent us off. That was my last meeting with him.

It was the afternoon of 15 May. Though I tried time after time, I could not get in touch with anyone in the leadership. Some cadres and I had set up camp in a dense area of a palmyrah grove in Mullivaikkal. Bullets kept whizzing by very close to us. At the time, the captain of the Sea Tigers' women's front came to our stations. We had been good friends from the beginning because we had joined the Movement at the same time. She shared some confidential information with me.

It seemed there was a plan for the Leader of the Movement and a few cadres to escape secretly. The Sri Lankan Navy battleships had tightly blockaded the Mullaitivu stretch of sea, and they could not escape through the ocean. I learned that they had determined to cross the Nanthikadal lagoon in small boats, fight the army stationed in the Keppapilavu area, create a pathway, creep through the Keppapilavu forest area and advance through the jungle.

It was openly understood that, given the Movement had neither the strength, nor the strategy to break the army's stranglehold, the probabilities of this plan succeeding were slim to none. As we were discussing the plan, a cadre who was in the know added: 'As they are moving through Nanthikadal, they will strike the army stations the moment they see them, and advance until they reach the jungle; that's the plan.' She told us that a male cadre who was in love with her had shared the information with her. That cadre, Imran, was in the Pandiyan brigade. I didn't know how credible this information was. Yet, I realized at that moment with utmost clarity that that the fighters had been abandoned. Never mind the dead, no one had been given any instructions as to what the fate of the injured or surviving fighters was to be. At this time the movie about the 300 warriors that the leadership had shown us came to my mind. In that moment it felt to me as though the leadership had decided the end of our fighting life a long time ago.

The Sothiya brigade troops had set up their station close to our camp. Only one or two fighters remained there. A senior fighter there told me that many of them had gone in search of their parents or anyone they knew or recognized. She was a fighter who carried out the vital tasks of the brigade. Her husband had been an important combat trainer in the Movement. A highly educated and skilful person, he was in a terribly heartbroken state because of the wrongdoings of the Movement. In a severely injured state, he had urged his wife to join the civilians and go over and surrender to the army. I learned that he had committed suicide afterwards.

I saw Brigadier Sriram of the Sea Tigers in a place where a large boat belonging to the Sea Tigers was kept. He had joined the Movement at an early age and grown to be a highly skilled brigadier. Whenever he saw me, he would affectionately call me akka as he talked. 'What's the situation, Sriram?' I asked him. 'What's left to do now, akka? We need to quietly leave with the civilians,' he said. 'The boys have gone to get some petrol to burn this boat; that's all I'm waiting for.' I asked him where his wife, Isaippriya was. He remarked that she was around somewhere close by and would arrive soon.

I kept trying several times to get in touch with my immediate superior Nadesan; I got no reply. It struck me that it was dangerous to retain the cadres who were still with me, expecting to hear from command. There were some injured cadres, some married cadres and a few others who were with me. I asked them all to put on ordinary clothing and go join the civilians and leave. Many of the combatants wailed openly. They must have felt like a family being separated and sent into the dark, where they had no idea what would happen to them. I stayed back trying to reunite the injured cadres with their families or acquaintances. As time went on, many managed to leave.

Purani and some cadres who were with him were stuck not knowing what to do. Purani had been badly injured in the leg and was unable to walk. Born in Chulipuram, he was a close relative of senior Tamil political leader Hon. Amirthalingam. Just like the Hon. Amirthalingam, Purani too was an eloquent orator. Purani's parents had died. His relatives had all migrated out of the country. 'We didn't come to the Movement because we didn't know how to earn a livelihood, we came to fight for the people. If we had lived like others, we could have lived well. What to do. How many people like us have we lost? We have given our arms and legs to the Movement and now we have no idea what to do,' he complained bitterly. Of the Movement's brigadiers, we were only able to contact Soosai. Purani got ready to go meet with Brigadier Soosai.

It was the 16th, and it was getting close to the afternoon. People were crowded onto Mullivaikkal road, ready to begin the journey to Mullaitivu. The cadres had been completely abandoned by the Movement's leadership, and they were completely ignorant of what was happening at the higher levels of command. The corpses of the dead were scattered here and there. We were at the juncture where no one could help the injured.

The cadres who were left alive had no option but to join the civilians and leave the area or kill themselves somehow. Under these conditions, thousands of fighters mingled with the crowds and got ready to leave. As a mother hen would tuck her chicks under her wing in times of danger, so the Tamil people affectionately embraced the fighters and took them in among themselves. Some people even picked up the few injured and abandoned fighters and carried them as they prepared to leave. While many fighters would have liked to leave, they hesitated and held back because their hearts were fearful of what might come next. Like a flood bursting through a dam and over the shore, the people came out in wave upon wave onto Mullivaikkal Road.

The fighters murmured among themselves that Brigadier Soosai had asked that the people be prevented from leaving until the evening. They also mentioned that one or two fighters had been stationed on the road for the purpose. In the early evening, the people pushed aside the few cadres stationed on the road, knocked them over and began to leave in waves. Who cared if anyone accepted it, or objected to it? I understood the truth, in that moment, that the Liberation Tigers' armed struggle had failed in the most terrifying way.

The crowd in Mullivaikkal began to diminish. The army's bullets kept flying over our heads. In a few hours everything would be finished. Only then did I realize I had been pushed into a situation where I had to come to a decision about myself. Do I bite the cyanide capsule? Do I commit suicide by shooting myself? I was caught in a battle between my heart and my head and I began to flounder. The life we had lived as one large family in the fight for freedom, the deaths of the all the fighters who had sacrificed their lives, and the courage to be prepared to die for our dream all weighed like iron in my heart.

In my soul I completely rejected the idea of surrendering to the Sri Lankan army who were our enemies. Though I knew that suicide was a useless death, I recognized that it was the character of the Liberation Tiger to be completely resolved to give up their life. Do I die to prove that I am a resolved and courageous fighter? Do I escape like a coward to save my own life? The tightness in my chest felt like it would explode, but only tears sprang up.

At the same time, intuitively I hesitated to accept a death by suicide. In that moment, my committing suicide felt like a completely useless gesture. I began to wonder what kind of safety I could expect, as a female fighter, if I decided to move forward into this next phase, when it was unclear what exactly this phase was, and what consequences I would have to face. My mind told me that it would require greater resolve to keep myself alive and get past the trials ahead than to kill myself because I didn't have the capacity to face the dark days ahead.

My own individual nature is such that my decisions have to take both my feelings and my intellect into account to a certain extent. I had not joined up as a fighter purely out of some emotional stirring. As an Advanced Level student, with the judgement I was capable of, under the circumstances of that time, I joined the Movement with the intention of serving my community. I believed that taking up arms and rebelling was the highest service I could perform for my people, in that environment.

I believed with my whole heart, that beyond the death of the individual fighter, there would be a transformative benefit to our community. I was completely willing to sacrifice my life for such a communal good. At that time, there was no room for other choices as the Liberation Tigers' Movement had gained the favour of the majority of Tamil people and was acting as a strong freedom Movement, and for that reason I too joined up as a Liberation Tiger.

I had joined the Movement with the dream of going into battle for the people's freedom, and I was given the opportunity of doing political work among the people in a way that I had never even dreamed of. I enjoyed working hard because I loved the people so much. It gave me joy to imagine a life where all people lived in peace and equality. I firmly believed the Tigers would win and that we would create such a nation. I had firmly resolved to sacrifice my heart, body, life and soul in the fight to that end. In the time that followed, through the experiences I had, the lessons I learned, the circumstances that led me to have faith in the Movement, the decisions that created a loss of trust, the actions that didn't prioritize the people, all combined to cause a momentous confusion within me, and pushed me to form my own opinions. However, like all the fighters, I too firmly believed that the Leader would not let the sacrifice of thousands of lives be in vain, and that he would mobilize any political gains towards creating a lasting peace for the people.

When the leadership decided on the final battle, from my admittedly limited perspective, it did not seem like a good decision. In the days following, the ways in which the feelings and lives of the fighters were manipulated for a war that could not be won, and the actions that belied the people's faith, were untenable not only to me, but also several other fighters, captains and brigadiers. However, bowing to the orders of the leadership and obeying them was the symbol of our principles and our faith in the Movement. We had been raised within that kind of military tradition. Just as Pottu Amman had said in our final meeting in Puthukkudiyiruppu, we had no option left but to obey the Leader's orders and have faith that he would somehow pull off a miracle.

On the afternoon of 16 May, I decided that I would leave, along with the fighters who remained. It is not easy to make someone understand the heart-wrenching pain that tore us apart flesh from blood as we left Mullivaikkal, because there are no words that could describe it. I have no memory of putting on an old salwar that a female combatant who was with me gave me and mingling with the civilians as we walked out. We felt ourselves carried up in the flood of people that overflowed the banks.

My 18 years of fighting, from 29 July 1991 to 16 May 2009, ended in that moment. It was terrifying to even think about what might come next. There were explosions thundering behind us still. The blackest columns of smoke kept rising to touch the sky. The final glances of the family, with whom I had shared my life on the battlefield, their eyes full of longing and a lifetime of pain, kept crashing and splattering within my chest like the great waves of the Bengal sea. It was hard for me to carry my own body, which felt like a lifeless corpse. The electric lights in the Mullaitivu stadium, which was filled with people, were burning as bright as the afternoon. The army surrounded the grounds. I too stepped into the next phase, which seemed like an abyss of darkness in my mind.

9

Surrender and the Prison Cell

The people moved like a river along Mullivaikkal Road, crossing Vadduvakal Bridge and heading towards the centre of Mullaitivu. The army advanced on either side of the road towards Mullivaikkal continuing their attack, avoiding the rows of people leaving. The army had taken several relevant security precautions, expecting the arrival of large numbers of people. It became clear that there had been a plan to securely get the civilians out in the final stage of the war. The fighters trembled with anxiety, wondering how the army who had stood across from us heavily armed only a short time ago would treat us now.

When we reached the Mullaitivu grounds it began to get dark. Barbed wire had been set up all around. Military personnel stood guard all around the grounds. The people began to gather in small groups here and there, finally gaining a reprieve from the flying bullets and shrapnel. Like a python, death had swallowed and coughed up these people. Like civilians among civilians, thousands of fighters had also surrendered our fate to the hands of the Sri Lankan forces and waited with conflicted hearts.

The army was giving out water bottles and food packets. I was seated with some fighters in a spot somewhere in the middle of the field. I was not in a state where I felt hunger or thirst. I was only tormented by the guilt of having committed a terrible crime.

The rumbling explosions we heard from the direction of Mullivaikkal had begun to die down very slowly. The faces of the fighters who had wanted to leave but had hesitated because of the fear of what would happen to them if they surrendered, haunted my mind. The army was busily engaged in attending to the needs of the civilians.

The next day dawned. The people, filled with anxiety about what would happen next, began to prepare themselves for the next stage. They had gathered their identity cards and other miscellaneous documents together. We had no documents with us. I could not remember where my Sri Lankan national ID card and passport had been abandoned. I had not kept them safe because I never thought I would have any occasion to use them again in my life.

The cadres who had come with me went off to search for their relatives or their own villagers and joined up with them. I despaired of finding my mother or my sisters' families and stood bewildered, not knowing what to do. Since the day I had lied to my mother and gone off to join the Movement at 18, it was only now that I needed a mother's protection again. My younger sister's husband somehow found me within that crowd. He hurried away and returned with my mother.

My mother, who had stayed in the war zone until the end, for my sake, had joined my sisters when they left, because she had thought she would never see me again. The moment she saw me in the Mullaitivu grounds, she embraced me and rained kisses on me and began crying and sobbing. She called upon all the gods she worshipped and asked them to keep protecting her child, who had somehow survived. With the peace of a woman who had found her four-year-old who had gone missing at a temple festival, she held me close to her chest. I shrank before my mother's love, with a guilty conscience.

She forgot her foot pain and all her fatigue and struggled through the crowds of people to receive the food parcel and drinking water distributed by the army and forced me to eat. From the time my father died, though I was the eldest daughter, I had never been a source of comfort to my mother. I had dashed my mother's hopes and brought her a lot of grief, and had been no use as a woman, even up to now. Even now, I had only joined her as a high-risk burden. I would not be alive today if my mother had not held on to my hand firmly, as if I were a small child who needed to be kept an eye on; she protected me by staying with me.

That afternoon was spent in the Mullaitivu grounds as well. Though the people were being let in in stages, they kept coming wave after wave. It was nighttime again, by the time my mother and I were done with the examination and allowed in. My mother and I spent that night too in the grounds, along with two other young women fighters. We spread a cloth on the bare ground, and after many years I lay safe and close to my mother, with the burden of my griefs pressing upon me like rocks and keeping me awake that night.

The next morning, the people were loaded into hundreds of trucks that were lined up along Mullaitivu Road. My mother and I got into one of the trucks. There were a few cadres and some children who had come from the Movement's care home. I felt confident that someone from one of the aid organizations would help those children. My heart burned, and I was unable to so much as look at the faces of these little ones who had barely escaped with their lives this time.

That convoy of vehicles stopped and lingered at many points during the journey. On 18 May 2009, we reached the Omanthai army examination station at around midnight. Once everyone was unloaded from the vehicle, we were all asked to sit in one area. Even at midnight, the electric lamps poured out a flood of light. Someone announced on the loudspeaker that the people were all being welcomed by the President of Sri Lanka, that the people had now been rescued after the long war had been won, that they no longer had anything to be afraid of, and so on to many other matters.

After a short time, an announcement was made: 'Anyone who was in the Movement get up and come forward; even if you were only in the Movement for one day, you must come forward.' My mother became very frightened. I had known for certain that the registration and procedures for former cadres would be different, so I comforted my mother. 'Don't worry about anything, amma. They'll send you to a civilian displaced persons' camp (IDP). Go reach there safely with thambi and thangacchi's families. I'll 'get in touch with you somehow amma, don't be afraid,' I said as I comforted her. Then I picked up my little bag and without hesitation got up and joined the line of people who had been part of the Movement.

I had no intention of hiding myself for my own safety. I was firmly resolved that acting with integrity in this situation would be the only thing that would save me. Once a certain number had gathered there, a guide came and took us to another location.

19 May dawned. As we walked a little further, we could see a large hall where thousands of people were seated. They were all Movement cadres. I could see that the men were being registered separately from the women. We were now in a place where we could not hear any more explosions; my heart felt wounded, and I ached from an unbearable grief when I thought of the many close friends we had left behind. Though everyone in that hall was from the Movement, my eyes scoured the place for any faces I knew very well. Yet, it did not occur to me to speak to anyone. Like me, many people sat there in a dejected silence.

All the data on the people who had been in the Movement was being carefully registered by the Army Intelligence Division personnel; individual photographs were taken as well. It took a long time to register each person in this way. Only the army personnel who were fluent Tamil-speakers had undertaken the registration. The afternoon passed as well. There were more new people arriving. The ones who had been registered were loaded up in trucks and sent to a different location. People there said they were being taken to rehabilitation centres.

I observed some Tamil youths running around doing errands for the army personnel. The humiliating manner in which some of them spoke to us was like a spear thrust into an inflamed wound. I reached such a point of bitterness I kept my mind in a state of coma. I had moved forward in that slow queue and reached the registration table. At that time, I heard someone call out to me in a familiar tone, 'Thamizhini akka … Thamizhini akka …' and I turned around. One of those Tamil youths signalled to me to get up and follow him.

There were two military personnel waiting with him. I went with some fear and hesitation, wondering what was going to happen now. I didn't hide the fact that I was Thamizhini and admitted it freely to them. They took me straight to the registration area. My full name, address, and the length of time I had served in the Movement were all recorded. I registered all my personal information with no attempt to conceal anything. They took my photo. I had the slim hope from the beginning that if I was at least truthful I would get the justice that was due to a prisoner of war.

After my information had all been registered, I was held separately on one side of the hall. I could see that the procedures were different for me. At that time, a high-ranking military official who had arrived came over to me and said 'Vanakkam Thamizhini' and began speaking in fluent Tamil. I was very shocked when I saw him. Cogs began to turn in my mind that I had seen this man and spoken to him somewhere. It only took a moment. Then it came to me like a bolt of lightning to the head. When journalists had come to Vanni during the ceasefire, he had come along as well, claiming to be the representative of some Sinhala media outlet. He had met with many of the Movement dignitaries, including the Political Aide, and had also met with me in Kilinochchi where the Women's Political Office was based.

Many memories came to me, of this man, who spoke Tamil so well, easily befriending and interacting with several cadres and captains with the ruse of being sympathetic to the struggle. Not only that, I remembered when the memorial for the first Maaveerar 2nd Lt. Malathi took place with great ceremony in Kilinochchi in 2004, he too had attended the event, introducing himself as a journalist and speaking very comfortably on numerous issues. I was awestruck when I thought of how cunningly this military intelligence officer had managed to throw sand in the face of the Tigers' Intelligence Division and roam about through the nooks and crannies of Kilinochchi. This was something I had personally witnessed that clarified for me the kind of tactics the army intelligence operatives had used to penetrate the Tigers' districts.

The military intelligence officer too realized that I had recognized him. He began to speak to me most respectfully.

'Thamizhini! You need not be afraid. We cannot send you along to the Rehabilitation Centres, like everyone else. We must interrogate you further, as you were a head in the Liberation Tigers' Movement. So, we will be handing you over to the CID. You will be subjected to legal proceedings,' he said.

After that, I was made to sit alone on the side of that registration hall for many long hours. I tried, as much as I could, to avoid thinking about what was to happen next. I sat there like an inanimate object, simply staring at what was immediately visible. I had completely lost the ability to take anything up to my brain and contemplate, analyse or decide upon it.

A Tamil youth brought one of the day's newspapers and showed the photographs to everyone there. They had released photos of the murdered leader. 'Your Leader is dead, everyone cry now,' he said, and he mockingly pretended to cry himself. A small sound escaped everyone in that hall and was contained in the same instant. It is very hard to describe the conditions when we heard of the death of this man, whom we had respected as an older brother, loved like a father, worshipped like a deity that had taken form before us, whom every single fighter held so firmly in our hearts, and whose words we thought of and acted upon as sacred. We heard, and yet all acted as though we had not. Every fighter's face there looked like a demon had struck it. To those who knew of the last plan the Leader had made, the news told us what must have happened in the Nanthikadal lagoon. And yet, no one opened their mouths to say anything. It must have occurred to us that as lone individuals it was best that we each now avoided worsening our own situation.

On the afternoon of the 19th, I was loaded on a bus that had been brought there. There were some male fighters on that bus already. The vehicle passed Omanthai and began heading towards Vavuniya. Two CID men in plainclothes were also in the vehicle. They kept looking at me and talking among themselves in Sinhala. The vehicle sped along and was eventually halted in an area dense with trees. We were all unloaded there and taken into a building.

We passed a hall with prison cells made of iron cages. I saw many young men crowded and locked up in those barred cells. One or two of them called out to me by name. As we were walking fast, I could not turn and look at them, but kept my head down as I passed them. It looked as though the men who had been brought with me were taken by a different entrance. Now I was taken all by myself to an office.

I was called into a large office where several military intelligence officials in plainclothes had gathered. One official showed me a large paper that looked like a poster. The photos of all the colonels and field division heads, including the Leader, were printed on it. There were many symbols on them. He specifically pointed to my photo. In it I was wearing a striped camouflage uniform and a cap. There was a question mark over the photo.

The officials asked me many questions in Sinhala and Tamil. I didn't understand Sinhala at all. I waited silently. Then, an official who spoke Tamil, began to talk to me. 'What happen to your leader Prabhakaran?' 'When you last meet him?' 'Some of the Colonels dead, do you know what happen to others? How you come in now?' They asked me all manner of questions. I could not give them a clear answer to any of their questions. I was not able to establish contact with anyone in the last days. They spoke something in Sinhala among themselves. Then they asked that I be taken away.

I was given a parcel of food for dinner, and a small bottle of water. They asked me to sit on a chair there and eat. I did not have the heart to eat even a handful of food at the time. I took the parcel saying that I would eat later. I was put into the same bus that brought me there and taken to the police station in Vavuniya. There, the police took down my information. Then I was locked up in a small metal cage where female prisoners were locked up. There were three women shut in there already. An elderly Sinhala woman warden lay asleep on a cement bench there.

I had been locked in a cage for the first time in my life. The women, who were getting ready to sleep, made room for me as well. They asked me what I was on trial for. LTTE, I said. 'Where did they catch you?' they asked. 'Anyhow, they'll take you to Colombo for investigation. Last time I was here they brought in a girl like this and the next day they took her to Colombo. You can get a good lawyer, fight your case and get out.' Saying this, they began to advise me as well.

I was amazed that these ordinary village women seemed to know the ins and outs of the law and seemed so casual about going in and out of prison frequently. They knew there was fighting in Vanni, but they had no idea about the current situation. They were chattering animatedly about how they would take revenge on their enemies when they got out of prison. From their conversation I gathered that they were there for getting into physical fights and brewing moonshine. Even at that time of the night, they kept chewing mouthfuls of betel leaf. In a state of mental and physical exhaustion, I lay huddled along the side of the wall. Even when my eyes closed in sleep I would wake up with a start. My heart pounded furiously.

Shortly after midnight, the door was opened in a hurry and three more women were thrust inside. The door was shut again. I was shocked when I saw who they had brought in. They were very well known to me. They used to work in the administration division of the Sothiya brigade.

'Weren't you sent to the rehabilitation centre? Then what happened to you?' I asked them anxiously. They told me since people were coming there in the thousands it was noisy and overcrowded there, and some arguments and fights had broken out between some of the girls there. When they had gone to try to talk with them and sort out the problem, a young woman who had been forcibly recruited began shouting at them and came to strike them. When the army realized the situation was getting out of hand, they sent them here. They were confused as to what would happen to them now.

At dawn, the warden took us in twos to wash. I bathed in the water trickling out of the single pipe there, in the little time I was given, and changed into the one dress I had with me. We were given a parcel of rice and sambal for breakfast. I felt terrible when

I secretly threw away the food that I had received the previous night into the garbage. My heart burned at the memories of civilians standing in a long line for rice porridge in Mullivaikkal. Even if hunger compelled me to eat, the stress I felt choked my throat and would not allow even one handful of food to go down. After a while, the Sothiya brigade women were called away. They told me they were being taken to a different rehabilitation centre.

On 20 May, shortly after noon, they asked me to come outside. One of the CID officials who had dropped me off the previous night had arrived. He wrote all my details on a report. He seemed very dignified in his manner. He told me that they were taking me to Colombo shortly, asked me to get ready, and left. I asked someone there for a plastic bottle and filled it with water. In the evening, I was put into a Pajero. There were two policewomen seated in it already. The vehicle drove to the same place where I had been to the previous night. In a little while Hon. Kaṇagaratnam, the Member of Parliament for Vanni district, was put into the car as well. His face looked pale, withdrawn and exhausted. As we could think of nothing to say under those circumstances, we remained in silence.

The vehicle began to travel towards Colombo. My heart quaked at the thought of the interrogations to follow. I decided to stop worrying about unnecessary things and thought I should take care to focus my mind. I had been very enthusiastic about meditation from my days in school, and even now I think of how helpful it was to me during that period of anxiety. I understood that I was heading towards a different time of crisis, one where I would not hear explosions. As midnight approached, the vehicle carrying us reached the notorious 'Fourth Floor' building of the Colombo CID.

When I saw the name board saying: 'Special Investigation Division', the palms of my hand and my legs became numb and cold. I had heard many terrifying stories about the 'Fourth Floor' when I was in the Movement. I grew dizzy and thought I might collapse wondering whether they were going to pull out my fingernails and toenails or hang me upside down. The people accompanying me seemed to be in some position of authority in the CID. They finished registering me in the office, and took me to the sixth floor, where they locked up female prisoners. I was handed over to the female CID officer who was on night duty there. Once she had given me a thorough physical examination, she put me by myself into a small cell with metal bars and locked it from the outside. There were a few more cages beside me. I could see the women who were in them wake up from their sleep and look around. They were all given strict orders not to talk to me.

The next morning, the girls there bathed and got themselves clean. I too had a head bath after many long days. The dust and grime in my hair from Mullivaikkal flowed black. The female CIDs were standing beside the bathroom door. I was taken for interrogation around 9 am that morning. First, a group of officials subjected me to questioning. Since I did not know even a word of Sinhala, the questioning was undertaken through an interpreter. Everything, from my birth to my first joining the Movement and to my final leaving, was recorded in that investigative report.

There were other women who had been arrested by the Terrorism Investigation Division held in the same area where I was held. They were later taken to Boosa detention camp. Many women from Boosa detention camp were brought to the Colombo Terrorism Investigation Division and then taken to be jailed in Welikada prison. They said that many hundreds of men and women from the Movement had been taken for further interrogation to the Boosa detention camp. Every day, my interrogations continued on some subject or the other. Some of the other women said that they had been beaten during their interrogation. But I was not subjected to any kind of physical attacks even to the end of my interrogations.

Representatives from the International Red Cross came by once a month to meet with the prisoners and distribute the necessities. To people like me, who had no contact with our family whatsoever, that help was a tremendous gift. They gave us each a notebook and asked us to keep them with us until we were released from prison.

I was subjected to a mandatory health examination by the CID. The young woman doctor who examined me spoke to me in what Tamil she knew.

'It's wrong to kill a living being. What a beautiful world this is. Why have you been a terrorist for so long? At least now, try to live with a love of living beings,' she advised. Her words wounded me deeply. Was I a rebel? Or a terrorist? I asked myself on what basis I had been turned into a rebel and then a terrorist. It was politics. It was also politics that indoctrinated us that only an armed struggle would help us gain our freedom. And it is politics that puts a stamp on you saying that you're a terrorist. As a child, didn't I have many dreams, ambitions and desires too? I too was raised to love other living beings from my childhood. Wasn't it the belief that I could secure my people's future by sacrificing my own life that drove me to join the Movement? But I too have been a cause of destruction and the loss of lives in the name of liberation. I thought it would be a betrayal of my conscience to deny or hide any of this.

While I was detained as a prisoner for interrogation, I was taken up before the judge once a month. We had permission to see one or two family members weekly. I could not send word to or get in touch with my mother because I had no idea which of the Vavuniya displacement camps she was in. As a result, I was not in contact with any family in all the four months I was detained in the Colombo CID investigative division. They too had no idea where I was or what had become of me. When I mentioned this to the International Red Cross representatives who visited, they told me they still did not have permission to go into the Vavuniya welfare camps.

I suppose my surrender must have been disagreeable to those who presented themselves as supporters of the LTTE. I learned of the many poisonous lies and fantastical stories that had been woven and spread about me, through the parents who visited the other Liberation Tiger prisoners. I was devastated when I heard these calumnious stories about how I had surrendered with millions in cash, or how I had gone to the Vavuniya civilian welfare camps with the military and identified many people to them. At first it was very hard to bear the thought that people I had held dear would retaliate against me for the sole reason that I had made it out alive, and not died in the final phase of the war. Many who served in the Movement with me know in their hearts that I have not done anything that would betray my conscience, and that I have not tried to save myself by betraying another cadre. But I understood that the slander and abuse were another stage I had to get through, and I accepted them in silence. I understood the kind of title that would be bestowed on fighters like me who escaped with their lives, by the crowds who clamour to survive by warming themselves in the heat of another's blood.

I only learned much later about the stories released in the media alleging that I concealed the fact that I had been in the Liberation Tigers' Movement and tried to hide myself in the Vavuniya welfare camp with my mother until the CID arrested me. These things did not bother me. Every form of registration had been undertaken during my surrender in Omanthai. So, I waited in the hope that the legal procedure due to a prisoner of war would be followed for me as well.

In the time that I was detained for questioning by the Colombo CID, between 20 May 2009 and 29 September 2009, I was living with people who had been brought in for all manner of investigations. Many men and women, including fake overseas agents, swindlers and suspected Tigers from all over Sri Lanka were held there. It was there that I got to know diverse people outside the circle of my family, the Movement and the Tamil community for the first time.

Many naive women had been compromised by the circumstances they had found themselves in. Some of the other women there were fearless and seemed handpicked for a life of crime. A day spent with them felt like an eternity. CID women stood guard 24 hours a day outside the cages we were shut in. They accompanied and stood beside us whether we went to the toilet or to bathe.

The women's detention area was suddenly shifted from the sixth floor to the fourth floor. A cage was assigned to us in the same area where the men were detained. We women, wondering how we were going to stay in a place without any privacy, began to use the mats and covers we had, to create a screen. Seeing this, the officials brought some sheets of Zip board in and created a proper cover for us.

I record this here because a woman who is sent to prison and returns is stigmatized in our society. There are people in our society mean-minded enough to ostracize women simply because they were taken in for questioning. The society that accepted women taking up arms for the struggle and praised them as heroines when they died by the thousands on the frontlines, considers them to be fallen women when they return from prisons or rehabilitation camps.

Even worse, there are self-centred individuals who are quite willing to let the honour of Tamil women fly in the wind for their own political gain. Apart from the sisters who were subjected to sexual assault in the final stages of the war, from the beginning of the struggle, women have been subjected to sexual assault and sexual harassment. People in the groups that set out to fight for liberation have also been involved in sexual misconduct. There were also some instances among the Liberation Tigers, when men who had committed sexual crimes were executed in front of a gathering of cadres.

The women of communities that go into revolutions or wars face not only the loss of life, but also these kinds of sexual assaults, time after time. Beyond this, when a woman goes out to fight, she keeps blazing within her the power to safeguard her own honour. When a female fighter stands on the frontline, she knows full well that she is in danger of losing not only her life but also her honour. And yet, she has bravely stood in the battlefield for the good of her people.

The society that is content to benefit from that sacrifice during the war, looks askance at her life after the war. The bodies of sexually assaulted women are displayed for political gains. What a low and disgusting thing it is to spread the opinion that all women who have participated in the war and escaped with their lives must have come back without their honour. I know thousands of fellow cadres who, in their lives as freedom fighters and in their terrible time in prison, have burned like fire and safeguarded their honour.

After the four months of my interrogation by the CID investigations division came to an end, they got a signed confession from me. After I received another medical examination report from the Legal Medical Officer, I was presented to the Judge in the Puthukadai (Aluthkade) High Court. On his order I was taken to be held in remand at Welikada prison. My prison life stretched out in the women's section of the Welikada cells.

It was past 7 pm when I was taken to Welikada prison. Around 10 of us who had been taken to trial that day and put into remand, were taken from Puthukadai Court to Welikada prison that day. Apart from a few words of Sinhala I had come to be familiar with during my four months in the CID, I didn't know enough Sinhala to carry on a conversation with anyone. All the women who were transported with me from the court to the prison that day were Sinhalese.

The blue truck with bars on the windows, and 'Prison' painted on the side, drove into the grounds of Welikada Prison. The first thing you see is the main building. That is where everyone is usually registered. You could see that the area where the men were jailed held thousands. The prisoners who had been given their sentences were clad in white uniforms. Some men had been brought in the same truck with us. Reeking of tobacco or their eyes reddened, intoxicated by ganja, the men were manacled and linked together by a long heavy iron chain as they were brought in.

The women were registered and then we were loaded into the same truck to be driven over to the women's section, which was close by. A different world stretched out behind those massive iron doors. As it was nighttime, all the prisoners had been locked in. The female naval officers who had been appointed to carry out the body search for the incoming prisoners searched me and my belongings. It was there that I first experienced the repulsive process of body searching that is just one of the hateful and torturous practices of prison life.

The doors of our prison cells were opened, and we were sent in. There was no place to put your feet, the place was so crowded. It was full of women sitting, sleeping, and chattering away. The prison warden put me in, locked the door and left. I stayed awake, standing, because I did not know what to do. There was a constant buzz of noise. A woman who knew me from before came forward and, taking my bag from me, walked me over to her spot. 'Stay here for a bit, I'll go and get the leader,' she said as she walked away.

Some of the women I had got to know while I was in the CID building in Colombo were also kept in remand here. They came running over to talk to me. They gave me biscuits to eat and a bottle of water. My stomach was burning, since I hadn't eaten all day. I ate hurriedly. They brought the leader over and asked her to assign a sleeping spot for the new prisoner. The leader was a Sinhalese woman, very short in stature. I later learned she was a drug dealer who had been in remand for many years.

She asked a woman there to make some space for me. The woman began shouting that there was no space beside her. The leader shouted back at her. Eventually they came to the decision to let me stay in that spot.

'Fold your clothes and use them as a pillow. They only give you a little space for a pillow. That's where you sleep, and that's where you keep your belongings as well,' the Tamil women there informed me. In addition to that, they also told me about the regulations I had to follow while in the prison. 'If you don't follow the rules properly here, you won't be able to bear the scolding and abuse you get. Watch how you behave,' they warned me.

I looked around fearfully. I didn't know how much longer I would have to stay like this. But in those two years and nine months, that prison was like a university to me, in teaching me a whole other side of human life. It was there that I learned the truth that a prison cell can make a person a great saint or a terrible villain. Many societies generally look on prisoners as a symbol of embarrassment and ostracize them, and as a result not everyone gets to have the opportunity to understand their motivations.

This is why they become their own isolated society, with their own ideas of justice and injustice, subjecting the world of the prison to their own governance, and establishing the boundaries for their own lives. The meanings embedded in the phrase 'Prisoners are people too' are very profound.

The first day I spent at Welikada, I was given sleeping space in Section 32. It was the section next to where I was seated. Just a line marked the boundary. The lines marking the sections were only the gaps created in the cement during construction to prevent cracks from forming. I moved into the next space. But it was a terrible struggle to find a place to sleep. When it was already such a problem for the prisoners there to find space for themselves, they were not happy to have to accommodate me. There was just one Muslim woman who could speak Tamil. The rest were all Sinhalese women. They did not want me, the new prisoner, to be sharing space with them, and so they kept taking turns in scolding the leader who had told me to stay there.

The women in that section also had their own leader. She did not know a word of Tamil; she communicated with me through hand gestures. She cleared a small space for me to sleep next to her. Each section was about eight feet wide. Six women had to sleep in that space. The slightly taller ones could not stretch out their legs when they slept. There was not enough room to sleep uncurled. You couldn't keep your hands by your sides when you slept. Even if you managed to fall asleep somehow, you couldn't do it without bumping into the person next to you. You couldn't turn in your sleep. Even if a mosquito bit you, you couldn't brush it off in a hurry. To sleep at all, with these conditions, was a great feat. I realized by the next day that it was usual for people to pick fights with those next to them.

Truly, it was no ordinary feat to learn the ins and outs of prison life and adapt myself to them. I was amazed to discover the level of patience I found within me. I learned to be silent no matter what anyone said to me. I would put my pillow to my head and sleep as straight as a rod. The strong electric lamps that turned night into day would be kept on until dawn. I would cover my face with a small cloth to find some release from the light that irritated my eyes. When I dozed off unwittingly, someone beside me would quietly scratch me.

'Sleep on a slant, there's not enough room,' she'd say. If I slanted a little, afraid that I would get a scolding if I didn't listen to her, the other one would shout: 'Don't lean, don't lean, sleep straight!' In the beginning I was terribly afraid. I would wake up with a start and sit up. Sometimes they would shout and fight even in the middle of the night. I would cover my face and sit huddled against the wall. I spent many nights without a wink of sleep, my eyes open until dawn.

The day after I got to the prison, they called me to the office and gave me a small piece of cardboard with my remand number, ward number and section number written on it. The dominance of the long-term prisoners held sway in the office as well. The female wardens had to be called 'nona'. Whether or not we behaved well towards the 'nonas', we had to behave well with the 'senior prisoners'. The new prisoners who didn't abide by that rule suffered for it. In practice, usually all the control of the prison is in the hands of the senior prisoners.

My arms and legs had grown weak from being shut in a small cage cell for months, and when I walked around in the prison yard for a short while, I was exhausted and in terrible pain for two days. It was only after I got to Welikada, after all that time of being in a cavernous building with no sense of sun or rain, that I smelled the outside breeze, as it passed over the high brick walls. It had been a favourite pastime of mine from childhood to stare at the nighttime sky. It soothed my soul to stare at the sky at dusk until they closed the metal doors. I felt as though the memories of the past floated around me like dark clouds that sucked away my life. I sought out solitude a lot. The sleepless nights wracked my nerves. With my relentless headaches and heavy heart, I began to wonder if I was slowly descending into mental illness.

Many Tamil women were detained there under suspicion of having aided the Tigers. There were many elderly women among them as well. As soon as the doors opened in the morning, they would rush to the crowded washing area and bathe, sprinkle holy water on themselves, put on sandalwood paste and kunkuma powder and go stand in the kovil doorway. These women who had treated the Liberation Tigers like their own children had been identified by those cadres and were arrested. Young married women were imprisoned as suspicious persons. In the time I was there, two women were detained with their children. A three-year old boy and a two-year old girl were suffering a prison sentence with their mothers. Apart from this there were many young women of marriageable age there who had no connection with the Liberation Tigers.

There were female cadres from the Movement who had been captured alive during various naval or ground attacks, as well as female Black Tigers who had been arrested in Vavuniya or Colombo when they had been sent there on Black Tiger operations. When I got there, only a few women from the Liberation Tigers' trials would speak to me comfortably. The majority kept away and let their feelings be known through abuse and threats. 'Why did she survive? These ones should have died. We trusted them and helped them and now we're here.' There were many who scolded me in this manner and took out the anger and disgust they felt towards the Movement on me. Some have used the most abusive language deliberately within my earshot. They had heard the defamatory stories that had been spread about me outside and believed them to be true, and I learned to remain silent and not say a word while they berated me.

Though I was not personally responsible for the imprisonment of anybody there, the Movement that I belonged to was entirely responsible. Just like me, they had been thrown in prison because they participated in the Movement's activities and because they had hoped to serve our nation. No matter how harshly they criticized me, I could not be angry or upset; instead I felt a great sorrow when I saw their condition. Yet, there were mothers and sisters there who, amidst all this, embraced me with tears in their eyes.

Many who had been brought in as collaborators for the Tiger Intelligence Division had been arrested by the Prevention of Terrorism Intelligence Division and the CID in the Tamil areas that were under government control, and in Colombo. Many of them had been sent for remand to Welikada after more than two years of being detained for interrogation at Boosa detention camp. They had no idea what would happen with their trials and were frustrated by having to go back and forth from the courts. They were informed of their court dates one after another, but there was no further progress. The ones who came from reasonably wealthy families were able to arrange high-priced lawyers, but a majority came from families who could barely afford to come and visit them. Some human rights lawyers had taken on the cases of those arrested in the Liberation Tigers trials.

When I met Vasanthi Sarma, who was born and raised in Nelliady of a Brahmin family, she was in a terrible state. Her husband was in Magazine prison and she was in Welikada, and their children were being raised in an orphanage. She was in late middle age and suffered from illness from the time she got to prison. On seeing this, many Sinhalese women were helpful to her on many occasions.

She was called 'Iyer Amma' by everyone, and she was very affectionate and spoke openly with me. It was impossible to fathom the crimes and motives that she had been accused of when she often said to me: 'Child, I have never seen a young woman from the Movement face to face before.' I could not provide a reassuring word to ease her tears. She had continuous headaches and would use very strong medication. Surviving on a daily diet of rice and lentils, and whatever vegetarian food she got, her health deteriorated, and she suffered from many ailments. Who could be held accountable for her misery?

The suffering of the women who had their children with them was not a small issue either. One woman had been arrested with her infant at the Omanthai checkpoint. Another had been arrested with her infant at the Anuradhapura bus station. The two of them were from very poor families. One woman's husband had gone missing during the war. Their other children were being raised by their relatives. In that environment, which was completely unsuitable for children, they were exposed to all manner of diseases and the children were unhappy as well. Some compassionate Sinhalese prisoners would get food, clothes and toys for the children from outside and helped them out a lot.

For many of the young women detained in the LTTE trials, the marriage plans that had been arranged for them by their parents had been disrupted. Many young women had been abandoned by their romantic partners as soon as they were arrested on grounds of suspicion and they suffered great emotional distress as well.

The cadres who had been captured alive during strike operations, or arrested, had been serving their long prison sentences without any contact with their families.

A young woman from Batticaloa who had been tried on suspicion of being a Tiger, ended up in prison and was so deeply psychologically damaged that she went insane. Her life was wasting away being kicked and beaten by all the inmates beside the washroom entrance. Another young woman from Jaffna was captured alive though injured during the battle between the Tigers and the Sri Lankan army in Mukamalai in 2001. Though she was psychologically sound when she arrived at the prison, after many years of no contact with her loved ones, she became depressed and anxious, and after a while began to deteriorate emotionally and became very abusive towards the other inmates. Finally, she was shut in solitary confinement with her hands and legs bound, and eventually shipped off to the Angoda mental asylum.

Altogether, in the time I spent in Welikada more than 70 women were detained in the prison on charges related to the Liberation Tigers. In the time following this, many decisions came down through the courts for most of them. Some were released. Some had their cases taken before the Supreme Court. Their cases were moved to the courts in the areas where they had been arrested. Some of the women, who did not want to waste any more of their lives in remand, began to plead guilty to the charges laid against them in the hope that at least this way they could be free after they had served the sentence.

At this time, Buvaneswari and Katthaayi, the two women from Batticaloa received five years of hard labour each after their cases took 13 years to be tried in the Supreme Court. People arrested under the Prevention of Terrorism Act were not allowed bail, so on that basis, the two women were kept in remand during the entire period of the trial. One of them got cancer and I heard she died in Welikada Prison in 2013, before she could finish her sentence and go home.

After 2010, hundreds of Tigers who had surrendered after the final war were brought from Boosa detention camp to Welikada jail. Many of them were sent to the Vavuniya rehabilitation camp after the appointed few days. Others, like me, were detained for long periods of time. It was the custom for the Colombo Hindu Congress to arrange boxes of clothing and some necessities to be delivered to the Tamil political prisoners on Thai Pongal and Deepavali. With the help of some members of the diaspora, the members of parliament from the Tamil Alliance came by and gave us clothing and miscellaneous necessities.

The girls there would fight angrily with them when they came. They would ask them 'What are you doing about our freedom?' and argue with them. Bound as they were by rigid and oppressive laws in how their cases were handled, even now Vasanthi Sarma, Sathya and others still live with the dream that they can gain their freedom through political pressure tactics.

Everyone had forgotten about the lives of the civilians who had been used by the Tiger Intelligence Division for attacks in the government-controlled areas. The Tamil prisoners' fate only seemed to be a subject of discussion around election time. Hundreds of young men languished in prison labouring under serious charges having lost their families and futures. There is no one who can be held accountable for them now.

A majority of the people in prison seemed to be there on drug-related charges. From the big bosses who sold drugs by the kilo, to the small fry who sold them by the gram, and smugglers who brought in drugs from overseas, hundreds of women were here on drug charges. Though many of them were Sinhalese women, there were Muslim and Colombo-area Tamil women there as well. They would refer to the drugs specifically as 'Thool' in Tamil, and as 'Kudu' in Sinhala. From my experience in prison, it is my understanding that the 'Thool' bosses never take drugs themselves. The food that was brought to them from their homes was quite splendid. You could tell when you saw one of them that she was a drug lord, because they were noticeably plumper, wore different outfits from time to time, and walked around with a liveliness and sense of self-importance. They were shown the utmost respect in the prison. Even the prison guards behaved amiably with them. They each had more than one case pending against them. Within a few months of being released on bail on one charge, they'd be back in remand on another charge.

There were many women involved in the drug trade within the prison as well. They had a variety of techniques to bring in whatever drugs they wanted, as well as cellphones and whatever accessories they required. One day, I was on my way to the bathroom for a wash at around 4 pm. Something flew over my head and landed 'plop' beside me. I quickly looked around and dashed out of there. This kind of sudden attack only took place on the battlefield. I wondered what this was and kept watching from a distance. A pound loaf of bread that had been wrapped in plastic lay in front of me; before I could blink an eye, a woman had picked it up. She was the underling to a major drug pin. I realized that some valuable materials must have arrived in that loaf of bread.

They would receive goods along with their food products from the supervisors in a pre-arranged fashion, and then cleverly conceal it in intimate places on their bodies. There were many people skilled at bringing back these kinds of items on their return from the courts. They would very dexterously bring these items through the body searches we underwent, where we felt like the very skin was being peeled off us. When they were unexpectedly caught, they would be made to kneel for hours in front of the offices. Sometimes they were beaten with a belt. At these times, these women, who were the underlings, would take the punishment or charge without betraying their boss. For this reason, they were specially taken care of by their boss. The items brought into prison in a multitude of ways were cleverly hidden in the toilet and under roof tiles.

The reign of the prisoners began after the roll call was taken at 6 pm, and everyone was locked up and the doors closed. Right in front of us, the women would sell drugs, charge their phones, talk on the phone, do drugs and have their fights. Sometimes, something that began as a small fight would turn into a huge brawl and go too far. When the guards outside heard a sound, they would come by and, standing outside the door, shout 'What's that noise?' They would reply, 'It's nothing, nona! Just one of the loonies acting up, we'll take care of it; you go, nona.' They would appease the guards and send them away and pick up their fights where they had left off.

The law of the prison was that only an official had the authority to open the door leading to the cells and not any of the ordinary guards. In addition, they had to go to the office to get the key to open the doors. This was a well-known fact to the senior prisoners. They seemed highly adept at keeping the prison regulations under their control.

The underlings were often drug users. They were usually rough and lean in stature, half-dressed in old and tattered clothing, mouth full of betel juice, and roaming about with vacant, drugged out eyes. Wherever they went, they threw their weight around, and you would hear shouts, cries or foul language. You could never tell what they were going to do next. Sometimes they would skip around in euphoria. Very often though, they would take drugs and go into a daze, crouched on the ground with their heads hanging down like sleeping chickens. Some became as thuggish as men when they were intoxicated.

These women had changed in appearance, changed in nature and changed in their humanity. They were such skilled thieves they could carve out your eyeball while you were awake or knock you over and snatch something from you as they passed. You couldn't reclaim what was gone. You couldn't argue right or wrong with them either. They would just yell abuses at you. Through a variety of circumstances, all kinds of women: very young ones, beautiful, educated women, fluent English speakers, and women who had not a whiff of education had become slaves to their addictions and lived here as if the prison was their world, because their families despised and rejected them.

Occasionally a whispered alarm would spread like wildfire: 'Tsunami is coming!' During those times, the women's eyes would bulge so wide they looked like they'd pop out. Rigorous searches were often carried out in the prison and contraband items would be seized. The women would run around desperate to find a place to hide their contraband. At those times, they would reach the summit of solidarity. Cellphones and drugs would all be secreted away.

I've heard it said that the one who has something suffers one pain, the one who has nothing suffers many pains. We had the same problem in Welikada. Those who had relatives who visited them every two months, or sometimes less frequently, had to make whatever they brought with them last until the next visit. Whether you had contraband or not, everyone's space was searched the same way. Flour and sugar would be dug through and poured out. From the bottom of the water bucket, to the lid of the water bottle, every object would be scratched clean and scrutinized. Every seam of a garment would be examined. A pillowcase and single polythene bag held our meagre possessions in the allotted foot-and-a-half wide space that was barely enough to curl up and sleep in. The guards would empty them out too.

It was past seven one night. We had spread out our clothes and gone to sleep. Apart from the women who secretly charged their phones at night, and the women who talked on the phones until dawn, everyone else was preparing to sleep. I was lying down too. Suddenly someone wearing shoes stepped on my feet. I jumped up at once. The prison police, who were called 'Banda police,' male and female, surrounded the prisoners' cells. There was no chance to hide anything and, over the next three to four hours, hundreds of cellphones, packets of drugs, and money were seized during the search. The women were furious that men had been included in a search operation carried out at night.

The next night, when the police arrived at the same time to carry out the searches, the women prisoners began to riot. They shut the doors and prevented the ones who had come in from leaving, and with whatever broomstick or bottle came to hand, they began attacking them furiously. The prison police who had come in to carry out the search had no way to run out, so they hid in the bathrooms. After a while the situation was contained. The next two days were extremely tense. After that, however, no more male police came to the night searches. The prison regulations were tightened.

I had turned into a zombie from the mental strain I experienced, the cruelties of the prison and the uncertainty of what would happen next. More than anything, I felt it was important to find some peace of mind. I understood that I would have to direct my mind towards something to ease the pressure I felt. I started visiting the temple that was inside the prison. I began to fast. A deeper understanding of the truth came to me.

Even ordinarily, it was very hard for me to stay hungry. Apart from the days during the struggle when we didn't have any food, or when we had food but had no time to eat, from my childhood on, I had found it impossible to stay hungry. It's not lightly that they say that ten traits disappear when you are hungry. I found comfort in abstaining from food for the whole day when I was in Welikada prison. As my stomach burned with hunger, I felt as though the pressures of my mind began to heal. When I curled up in a corner without eating, or speaking to anyone, with an emptied mind, I felt I reached an infinite peace. On many occasions, the mothers and sisters who were affectionate towards me went in search of me all over the prison grounds after not seeing me in my assigned space, and they found me in the rear of the temple, or some other solitary spot. For some time, I could not stand to see people or talk to another human being.

During this time, I was switched to a section that held predominantly Tamil prisoners. Two of the prisoners there were from Black Tiger units that had been sent on strike missions and had been captured in 2007. One of them, Pavalam, a female cadre who had been surrounded by the army as she headed towards Jaffna for an attack, had been arrested just as she bit down on her cyanide capsule. She was given medical attention by the Terrorism Prevention Intelligence Division and sent to Welikada by the court after interrogations were completed.

The other, a Black Sea Tiger called Anbuvathani, had been stationed in Trincomalee for a strike operation. She was arrested by the Terrorism Prevention Intelligence Division, brutally interrogated at Boosa detention camp and then sent to Welikada prison.

I went with these young women to Christian worship and bible readings. I truly felt as though that space was a balm to my wounded heart.

With the help of a Tamil woman who had a cellphone, I was able to speak to my sister and get in touch with my mother. My family, who had no knowledge of what had happened to me, or where I was being held after I had been separated from my mother in Omanthai, had become very discouraged by the lies and rumours spread about me by the media. It was around October in 2009 that my mother came to Welikada prison to see me.

It is a very difficult thing to meet your family in prison. They would have to travel a whole day, arrive in Colombo, carry whatever necessities they had brought for us through the scorching afternoon heat along the tar road inside Welikada, stand waiting in a long line to have every item they had brought (including food parcels) taken apart bead from nail and thoroughly searched, before they were called in. You could only see them through an iron fence that was so tightly nailed in you could not stick your little finger between the fence and the ceiling in that small space. That dark room, with no lights, was always crowded with people.

You had five minutes maximum. Depending on the number of supervisors, that time could be shortened further. In that short time, they would only hand over the items brought over for us after digging through and scattering everything one more time. Sometimes they would even turn back food that had been cooked and carried over those long distances, refusing to give them to us. One person could not hear another over the constant buzz of noise. You would have to shout over it. You would have to peer through the fence in that darkness to even see each other's faces. It was the same procedure for the prisoners who got their food delivered daily from home; and it was the same situation for prisoners who only saw their relatives once a month, or once a year.

There were many human hearts that yearned for a handful of home-cooked food there, whom no one ever came to visit. I could not understand the expectations of those people who stared at the supervised meeting area from dawn to dusk, until the supervisory period was over, knowing full well that no one was coming to see them. The painful longing that spills over in the eyes of abandoned people in prison is a great torment.

Living so closely among Tamil, Sinhalese and Muslim women in Welikada, brought me many different experiences. I had never had the opportunity, in my childhood, to get to know people of different races. Once, during the peace talks, the parents and families of the missing army soldiers came up to Kilinochchi to meet with the Liberation Tigers' representatives. The tears of the aging Sinhalese mothers melted my heart. Tears poured from my eyes too. I am not ashamed of it. The tears and wailing of the Tamil mothers who had lost their children in the war came to my mind. Human beings can differ in race, language, religion or politics, but everywhere in the world, the general nature of motherhood is the same.

I cannot forget in my lifetime, the kindness of some of the Sinhalese mothers who became acquainted with me. It is through these close relationships that I began to learn to speak the Sinhala language. They would share their joys and sorrows with great sensitivity. They had many good opinions about Tamil people. Yet, ordinary Sinhalese women believed widely that the Tigers murdered Sinhalese people. Once they got close to you, they would come forward to help you in a crisis with no thought for themselves. The tendency to hold grudges was very rare among these people. Being around them, I was able to experience and understand the many good qualities which drove them to sate another person's hunger before they hoarded anything for themselves.

I was taken once every 14 days to the Supreme Court in Aluthkade for my case. My poverty-stricken mother struggled to arrange a lawyer for me. Though she had approached a Human Rights organization many times, for some reason they had refused to take on my case. For about a year, while I was in remand, I had no lawyer appear for me in court. 'Don't you have a legal representative?' they would ask, and I would answer 'No'. Though I was a fighter in a powerful movement, I had been abandoned because I had surrendered. It was not only me, but many thousands of other fighters who were in the same situation.

My mother arranged a lawyer for me with my sister's help. He was a good man, with great compassion. Though we had not given him any money, he, and his colleague Manjula Pathirana, a Sinhalese lawyer, came to the courts on my behalf many times. I knew that they could not effect any immediate change in my case. But at that time, they gave me some sense of confidence.

A miraculous change occurred in my case, which no one had expected. The CIDs who had interrogated me, had signed an agreement to have me sent for rehabilitation. The Sri Lankan government's decision to offer a general pardon to those who had surrendered, and rehabilitate them, saved the lives of thousands of fighters, and saved them from the vice grip of the law as well.

On 22 June 2012, the Colombo Aluthkade Court judge Rashmy Singampuli ordered that I be freed after a year's rehabilitation exercises in Vavuniya Rehabilitation Camp. On the order of the Court, I was sent from Welikada prison to the Vavuniya Poonthottam Rehabilitation Centre on 26 June 2012. The phase of darkness and disorientation had come to an end.

10

Rehabilitation

On 26 June 2012, I was taken to the Vavuniya Poonthottam Rehabilitation Centre. I learned that the Rehabilitation Centre was run by the Prisons and the Sri Lankan Army under the Bureau of the Commissioner General for Rehabilitation. I felt very uneasy at the time. I was afraid of how I would be treated. Though the Sinhala I had learned in prison would be somewhat helpful to me, the fear lingered that the army personnel who had been directly involved in the war would be abusive or vengeful in their behaviour towards me. Once they had examined all the documents pertaining to me from Welikada, I was admitted into the care of the Rehabilitation Centre.

I was taken to the office of the military official who was the liaison for the Vavuniya Rehabilitation camp. The official explained the regulations of the rehabilitation camp to me. 'You must coexist peacefully with the other women here, as you would do at home. It is unnecessary to discuss their past with anyone here. It is our hope that you will complete the rehabilitation exercises well and be reintegrated into society.' He asked me if I had anything to say. 'Any media releases about me while I'm here, or any meetings with the media will create complications for me,' I said to him. 'No media persons can meet with you without your consent,' he remarked. That was, on its own, a huge relief to me.

With BBC representative Frances Harrison in Vanni

The rehabilitation centre operated on the grounds of the Cooperative School. Sixteen women lived in a large dormitory. After being trapped in the overcrowded conditions of Welikada, it was a great comfort for me to come to this place. I began to participate in my rehabilitation exercises with the sense that I could leave this place in exactly one year. The women who were already there were affectionate and acted familiar with me in many ways. Several of them were younger than me. It made me very happy to be among them. I have always felt enthusiastic about getting to know younger people. Some of them would complain that they had aged and would express their frustration and disappointment. I had never felt those kinds of frustrations. I believed that keeping your mind strong and learning to renew yourself would keep you young.

The entire day, from morning to night, was packed with programming at the rehabilitation camp. We had training classes and tasks during the week, meditation exercises on Friday mornings with the 'Om Sakthi' organization, Christian worship on Sundays and no time to pause. In the time I was there, they conducted six months of sewing lessons. They also conducted three months of computer training, four months of training as aestheticians, and English and Sinhala classes. On top of this, workshops were conducted in business management, dairy product manufacture and psychological support. Many young women participated very enthusiastically in these classes. A few participated reluctantly, because they had no choice.

Weekly family visits were arranged here. They could come in at nine in the morning and talk until four in the afternoon and leave. We could receive things like food, clothing and other items, except for cell phones. The items were registered at the entrance and were allowed in only after they had been examined. My mother had made it a habit to visit me twice a month.

Once the news got out that I had been allowed rehabilitation, all manner of aspersions began to arise. I did not suffer the same kind of misery as when I had first encountered slanders shortly after I had surrendered. I learned to weigh people's intentions by seeing where the criticisms came from, and on what basis they criticized me. I could say that the bible verses about the eagle, which is called the royal bird, strengthened my heart a great deal. Its wings had the strength to fly against the wind. I began to feel determined that just as the eagle renewed itself and arose to fly with new strength, I too would strengthen myself.

The military officers running the rehabilitation camp, including the officer in charge of the women's division who was a Major, were fair in their practices. I cannot forget that Captain Jayani Herath, one of the female officials, treated the women there as if they were her own children. At the same time, she was very firm in maintaining discipline and following the rehabilitation regulations. She had been a teacher before she joined up for military service, and you could see the traits of a teacher in her still. She was as friendly with me as she was with the others.

She demanded that we keep our belongings in perfect order in the dormitory where we stayed. There were one or two girls who were not so orderly, and if she saw their belongings scattered here and there, she was in the habit of throwing those belongings away. One time, apparently, footwear had not been neatly arranged at the front entrance, and she picked them up, threw them far away and walked off. This was something that had happened before I got there. So, whenever the girls saw her at a distance, they would say 'The tsunami is coming!' One night, some of the women beside our dorm were sitting with us in a circle and eating our dinner. Suddenly, we heard someone call out 'Girls, the tsunami is coming… ah.' The tone sounded different, so we peered through the window and began laughing. Captain Herath had called herself 'tsunami' to make us all laugh. The other military women also treated us like good friends. The female military personnel joined in all the tasks that the women in the rehabilitation camp did, including cutting grass with a throwing knife. It was plain to see that the military personnel had been well trained in communication and psychology for the rehabilitation programme.

The rehabilitation camps for men had been established in Vavuniya and Welikanda. As the numbers being sent for rehabilitation were low, the men were switched to the Poonthottam rehabilitation centre as well. When more than a certain number of people had completed their rehabilitation period, it was customary to hold a grand ceremony where they would be handed over to their parents. Two such 'release ceremonies' took place in the time I was there. At each event, more than a hundred former cadres were handed over to their families.

In 2013 a sports contest and arts event were held for the April Tamil and Sinhala New Year festivities, in the Vavuniya Municipal building. The Minister for Prisons, Rehabilitation and Resettlement and, through his arrangement, some university students from Galle and Matara as well as some political dignitaries were present. They walked up to me and said: 'We want to talk to Thamizhini who is being trained here. Could you point her out to us?' A girl who was standing beside me blurted out, 'She is Thamizhini akka' without any thought whatsoever. The students who surrounded me began whipping their questions at me one after the other. I fumbled, not knowing what to do. The male and female military officials who were in charge of us saw this happen and immediately came over.

The students were bombarding me with questions about the Leader and about the Movement's past activities. I stood silent in the middle of that crowd. The military officials who understood my difficult position intervened: 'She is now undergoing rehabilitation. You can freely ask her any questions you have about that. However, we cannot permit you to ask her about her past and upset her.' The questions stopped with that. 'We're only interested in hearing about her past,' they said. The officials replied: 'You cannot bother someone who is undergoing rehabilitation by asking them questions about a past that will bring back memories for them. Even those who fought in the war until yesterday are thinking differently today. Only we keep raking up old issues.' I listened to what they said in silence.

On 23 October 2012, a wedding ceremony took place in the Vavuniya Rehabilitation Centre. The marriage was between a young woman named Priya, who was undergoing rehabilitation at the time, and a young man named Mathi, who had finished his rehabilitation and been released. Priya was a motherless child who had been abandoned by her father because she was a girl and was raised from her infancy by her relatives. She joined and served in the Movement. Later, as a result of a heart condition, she left the Movement and worked in the food manufacturing factory belonging to the Movement. She surrendered to the army after 2009, and after being detained in Boosa for interrogation was sent to the rehabilitation centre by court order. As the time of her release grew closer, a problem arose: into whose care could she be released. It was the custom to release someone into the care of their families or close relatives after their rehabilitation was over. If the former Tigers were to engage in any illegal activities after their release, the people who had taken them into their care would have to answer for it.

Though the mother of Mathi, the young man she was in love with, came forward wholeheartedly to take responsibility for Priya, the law would not allow it, as they were unmarried. As a result, the officials decided to hold their wedding in the rehabilitation centre. Priya was much younger than me, but she was a very close friend. Mathi, the young man she married, was a young man of many excellent qualities. He had lost one of his legs in the struggle. His family wanted very much to be of help to Priya. As this wedding took place in the rehabilitation centre, all the women who were present at the centre attended the ceremony. I learned that there were news articles accompanied by photos that came out claiming that I had played the role of bridesmaid in their wedding. The truth was that the groom's younger sister had been the bridesmaid. I laughed when I heard this story.

On 2, 26 and 27 of April 2013, the Ministry of Prisons, Rehabilitation and Resettlement organized a tour called 'Friends of Peace' for the people undergoing rehabilitation. The journey began as a convoy of more than 20 trucks. We first visited the Sri Lankan Parliament building. Minister Chandrasiri, who had arrived there, said to me:'Thamizhini! You must come to this place as a Member of Parliament.' I just smiled and kept walking in line. Whenever he saw me, during my time in rehabilitation, he would keep insisting 'You must go into politics, Thamizhini.' He was from a Leftist party. He became very close-knit with the former fighters who were undergoing rehabilitation. During an event that occurred in the Vavuniya Municipal Building, he once pointed out to me the fact that many from the Janatha Vimukthi Peramuna (JVP) Movement had left their armed struggle and turned to democratic politics. If I had consented to it, I could have joined their Leftist party and been active in it. But at the time, I did not enter any kind of political activity.

On the first day of our tour, we did our sightseeing at the parliament during the day and went to a special *bhajan* that was organized for us at the Sathya Sai Baba institute in Colombo. We were all given some delicious vegetarian food and gifts. That night, we were hosted at the travellers' hostel belonging to the Buddhist temple beside the Panagoda army base; the men on one side and the women on the other. Female military personnel and female military officials stayed with us as well. The next morning, we drove down the newly built highway to the Galle Municipal Council Complex. The first truck, marked with an 'A' was assigned to us, as the women were fewer in number. The Galle Municipal Council had organized a welcome event for us, called 'Welcoming Former Combatants into Society'. After that, we were taken for sightseeing to the Galle Fort. It was the first time I was seeing the sea and the waves since 2009. The sea of Mullaitivu and the many faces I cannot forget moved as a procession through my heart.

Thamizhini being welcomed by Sinhalese mothers when taken to Galle with the Rehabilitation Centre in 2013

After this, we were taken to the Deniyaya district. It was a beautiful part of the hill country, containing tea, rubber and other such estates. It's undeniable that the mountain breeze carrying the coolness of this lush greenery, gently caressing you in passing, and the 'sala' of the rushing Kalu ganga are natural wonders that could heal any wounds in your soul. A welcoming event was held in a Sinhala village there. Some elderly women brought us betel leaves in keeping with the Sinhala tradition, and little children brought us bunches of flowers to welcome us. Though the event was really organized for political purposes, the compassion rising in our hearts and the hearts of the people who surrounded us with smiles and welcomed us with embraces, and the tears that welled up in our eyes, were expressions of true human feeling that cannot be closed off and hidden away. A hundred-year-old political enmity cannot be settled by one or two moments of connection like this. But human feelings of compassion must be shared beyond ethnicity, language and religion. If human beings developed such an expansive emotional maturity, the world would be a haven of calm and peace. But what can we do? When the arms dealers of the world release the white doves, peace flies away with them and disappears. Of that entire sightseeing programme, the only thing that filled my heart was the love of those villagers.

We finished that day's continuing Hindu, Buddhist and Christian services and the evening's cultural events and spent the night at the Deniyaya Tamil school. Many Tamil people lived there as well. They were also very kind to us. The next day we had cricket and volleyball matches between teams of people undergoing rehabilitation and teams made up of the students and youths of that area. After that, we began the journey towards Kathirkamam. We reached greater Kathirkamam and stopped by the Buddhist vihara to offer our respects. We stayed that night at the hostel for Kathirkamam pilgrims and left the next morning for Sella Kathirkamam. Memories of roaming about Kathirkamam as a child, with my maternal grandmother, and of bathing in the Maanikka ganga swirled as dim memories in my mind. After this, we were taken to the newly built Mahinda Rajapaksa airport in Matale. The rehabilitation Commander Darshana Hettiarachchi and Minister Chandrasiri participated fully in this sightseeing tour.

I can never forget that during the time I was in prison and in rehabilitation, my younger sister's family and some dear people who were close to me helped out my mother when she was in financial need. My mother, who had moved from the Vavuniya detention camp and returned to Paranthan, found a cheap place to rent and began to live there. As my siblings were all married and living with families of their own, my mother kept insisting that I should get married as well. In my life before that, I had not given marriage any great importance, or much thought at all. It's not that I was determined to never get married either. I had no objections to marrying, if I met a helpmate who was able to understand my past life in any depth.

A friend of mine who lived in Germany began looking for a husband for me, along with my younger sister. I was very ambivalent about this at the time. It is customary in Tamil society to raise a girl from her childhood in preparation for her marriage one day. The usual reprimands of 'You're a girl, you should act this way' were never directed at me by anyone in my family. Instead, I was raised with a lot of love and freedom. I joined the Movement to fight for the freedom of the nation, but never misused my freedom and caused my elders any hurt.

I had every opportunity to get to know thousands of men during my time in the Movement. I created certain boundaries for myself, so that I would not be governed by any unnecessary feeling beyond the duties I was assigned. Many have seen me in my camouflage uniform and thought me a proud and arrogant woman and condemned me in those terms. 'Such women don't marry because they're ambitious for rank and power. Who would see such women and want to marry them?' they have said about me, to my own friends. Some others would give me advice secretly: 'It's not good to overtake the boys when you're riding your motorcycle' or 'It's not nice when you get up on stage and wave your arms around when you talk'. It is not just me, but many female cadres who have had these experiences. Occupied with our efforts for the Movement, we let such words that slid into our ears glide off into the wind and kept moving.

I had no great expectations that in our present-day society I would find a companion who could meet my expectations. I didn't know if I could bow to pressure and accept the role of a wife, sweep the house, cook a variety of dishes, wash clothes, go to the temple and observe fasts and live my life as a doll. Neither did I have the strength to have ego competitions with a husband who considered me his life's half and lose whatever peace of mind that remained for me. My family was not so wealthy as to buy me a husband with a large dowry either. I thought it would be the greatest comfort to live together with a deeply understanding, friendly soul, and share a limitless love.

The end of my rehabilitation period was approaching. Like everyone else, I too thought about my freedom with joy, and life in society with some anxiety as I counted the days. On 26 January 2013, Mr. Jayakumaran, who would later become my husband, spoke to me on the phone for the first time. Truly, I had not expected to speak to him that day. We talked continuously; we wrote each other letters. I came to love him deeply because of his open, easygoing and simple nature, and his understanding of my past and my future. It was only as I got to know Mr. Jayakumaran that I came to understand many things about love and family life.

On 26 June 2013, the head of the Vavuniya Rehabilitation Camp, Major Namal, handed me into the care of my mother. I had been released into society after many years. But I could not enjoy that freedom. The media published reports that I had supposedly been released in time to participate in the 2013 Northern Provincial Elections. I wanted to retreat somewhere quiet without the pressure of work burdens for a little while. I did not want my friends or loved ones to undergo any trouble or suffer threats because of me. On 29 September 2013, I got married in a simple and sweet civil ceremony in the presence of a few relatives. My husband, who turned out to be more of a soulmate than I had hoped for, became a great support for me. With his help, I overcame the guilt that often incapacitated me, and gathered the courage to face the challenges of the world once again.

With her husband Jayakumaran, at their wedding

GLOSSARY

FAMILY AND RELATIONSHIPS
Akka: Older sister
Amma: Mother
Ammamma: Maternal grandmother
Anna: Older brother
Appa: Father
Maama: Maternal uncle
Periyappa: Father's older brother
Thaatha: Grandfather
Sinnathaatha: Grandfather's younger brother

OTHER WORDS

Black Tigers: Referred to as 'Life Weapons,' this was a wing created within the LTTE that engaged in asymmetric warfare for strategic military gains at heightened risk to their own lives. Though often referred to as 'suicide bombers,' they differ from the conventional understanding of that term, as suicide was not an ideological aim in and of itself.

Eezham: An ancient Tamil name for the island now called Sri Lanka, it was used from the 1980s on to refer to the Tamil homelands, the territory demanded as a separate state by LTTE. It is also transcribed as Eelam.

EROS: Eelam Revolutionary Organization of Students was formed in London in 1975 by A. R. Arulpragasam, V. Balakumaran, K.I.B. Iyer, N. Thirunesan and V. Ratnasabapathy to develop the ideological groundings for a Tamil liberation movement. Many of its members were later absorbed into various rebel groups, primarily the LTTE, as well as other political groups. The name was later changed to Eelam Revolutionary Organizations, though the acronym was kept.

Kathirgamam: The site of a renowned temple dedicated to the Tamil God Murugan. It has become a pilgrimage space of syncretic devotional practices of people from multiple religious faiths.

Kumarappa and Pulenthiran (Shankarappa's brothers): Members of the LTTE, who were captured unarmed along with ten other cadres in a boat in Sri Lankan territorial waters. The arrest was controversial, as it took place during the Indo-Sri Lankan Peace Accord in 1987. All twelve captured cadres took cyanide upon learning they were to be transported to Colombo for interrogation, and only two survived.

Kumuthini Boat Massacre: An incident in May 1985, where 36 Tamil civilians were killed allegedly by Sri Lankan Navy personnel. Eye witness accounts collected by Amnesty International have documented the brutal hacking to death of men, women and children who were on the ferry 'Kumuthini' (also transcribed as Kumudini) travelling between the smaller islands of Neduntivu (also known as Delft) and Nainativu, close to the northern province of Jaffna.

Maaverar (Great Heroes): The term used to refer to deceased LTTE cadres who were killed during the war.

Muthukumar and Senkody immolation: K. Muthukumar was a journalist and intellectual from Tamil Nadu, who immolated himself in January 2009 outside the state Congress headquarters in Chennai, to protest the killings of Tamils in Sri Lanka. Senkody was a young woman in Tamil Nadu, who immolated herself in front of a township office in Kanchipuram in August 2011 to protest the death sentences meted out in the Rajiv Gandhi assassination trial.

Parai drum: Drum made of cowhide, the name refers to a historically oppressed caste from which the village or town criers were drawn.

Puttu: Staple made from steamed millet or rice flour.

Santhan: Santhalingam Gunaratnam was a popular Eezham Tamil singer recruited by the LTTE to perform songs related to the Tamil liberation struggle. Many of these songs were written by the renowned Tamil poet and propogandist Puthuvai Ratnathurai.

Shall we 'get married?': Euphemism for sexual intercourse.

SIRHN (Sub-committee for Immediate Rehabilitation and Humanitarian Needs): An institution created during the peace process brokered by Norway in 2002, by the LTTE and United National Front (UNF), headed by then Prime Minister Ranil Wickremasinghe for restructuring and rehabilitation. The plans fell through when the LTTE sought complete control over the reconstruction and development in the north and east, and the Sri Lankan government was unwilling to allow its own powers to be eroded in those areas.

Thamilselvan: Suppaya Paramu Thamilselvan, was the head of the LTTE's Political Wing, Commissar, and Political Aide to V. Prabhakaran until his assassination in 2007. His name is also transcribed as Tamilselvan and Tamichelvan.

Thevaram and Thiruvasakam: Parts of the Thirumurai (Holy Division) of 12 texts that form a collection of poetic devotions to the god Shiva. They were composed in Tamil in South India, between the 9th and 11th centuries. These two books are the most commonly used texts in the Saiva tradition in the Tamil homelands.

ABOUT THE AUTHOR

When **Thamizhini** was a student at the Parandhan Hindu Mahavidyalaya (1991), she joined the Liberation Tigers of Tamil Eelam (LTTE). Having acquired much combat experience even as a young woman, she later became a functionary in the women's section of the LTTE's political wing. As a leader, she earned the respect of LTTE chief Prabhakaran, leaders like Anton Balasingham and Adele Balasingham, and the people she served. She participated in several high-level meetings and events that happened during that period, and interacted with several national and international leaders and representatives.

ABOUT THE TRANSLATOR

Nedra Rodrigo is a co-founder of the Tamil Studies Symposium at York University, and an external researcher at the York Centre for Asian Research. She is a Spoken Word artist who has been featured at Scream in High Park, Desh Pardesh and Masala Mendhi Masti, and whose poetry has been published in various anthologies. She has translated works by R. Cheran, V.I.S. Jayapalan, Puthuvai Ratnathurai, Rashmy, Kuna Kaviyazhakan and others. Her essays have been published in the *International Journal of the Humanities, Global Tensions, Global Possibilities*; *Human Rights and the Arts: Essays on Global Asia*; *Studies in Canadian Literature* and *C Magazine*. Her translation of Kuna Kaviyazhakan's 'Forest That Took Poison' was shortlisted for the inaugural Global Humanities Translation Prize. She is the host of the bilingual, inclusive reading series 'The Tam Fam Lit Jam' in Toronto.

The Women's War is the gripping true story of a Danish female soldier's tours to the Helmand Province in Afghanistan. There she comes into contact with the Afghan women who are fighting against oppression, domestic violence and the horror regime of the Taliban, and together they initiate a covert collaboration. This is a book by a woman in the armed forces about what war does to women, about the looming risk of taking chances in wartime and about grief over fallen friends, but more importantly, it is about how women in one instance found the will to not only survive but to make something out of the terrible conditions that war brings.

A true account of the war against the Taliban—from the perspective of Afghan women

For special offers on this and other books from SAGE, write to marketing@sagepub.in

Explore our range at www.sagepub.in

PAPERBACK
9789353886301